Privil

Privileged Gifts

Motherhood and Marriage

Anne Dearing

Marshall Pickering

Marshall Morgan & Scott
3 Beggarwood Lane, Basingstoke, Hants, RG23 7LP, UK

First published 1986 by Marshall Morgan & Scott
Publications Ltd
Part of the Marshall Pickering Holdings Group
A subsidiary of the Zondervan Corporation

British Library CIP Data

Dearing, Anne
Privileged gifts: marriage and motherhood.
1. Christian life
I. Title
248.4 BV4501.2

ISBN 0-551-01377-8

Typeset in Plantin by Brian Robinson, Buckingham
Printed in Great Britain by Hazell Watson & Viney Ltd
Member of the BPCC Group, Aylesbury, Bucks.

Dedication

To my darling husband Trevor and my precious children, Rebecca, Ruth, Rachael and Philip, with my devoted love.

Acknowledgements

I would like to thank my husband Trevor for his help in producing this book, and Joan Popplestone, a dear Methodist friend in Plymouth, for doing all the typing. I would also like to express my gratitude to all who have been gracious enough to seek my ministry and all who have enriched my life with their love and friendship, for their contribution to the story told in these pages.

I pray that this book will bring glory to God who I serve and to whom I am so grateful for all His blessings.

Contents

Introduction

Many people in England and America have asked me over the years to write a book. I have hesitated to do so for two reasons. The first is that I am by no means a gifted writer; the second is that my story seems so relatively ordinary. However, my husband Trevor has now found time to help me put my story into writing, and I have been persuaded that many of the events of my life would be of interest to readers, simply because I feel I am an ordinary woman, seeing my role in life as primarily that of a Christian wife and mother.

I hope that all Christian women who read this book will find it profitable. However, since it was God's will that I married a minister of religion, I hope that women in a similar position may be helped as I relate my personal experience and the things I have learned through fulfilling this role. If they can persuade their husbands to read this book, then I hope they too may gain deeper insight into the needs of their wives and be the more able to understand some of the particular stresses of marriage to a full-time Christian worker. It is my prayer that with this insight their marriage may flow even more beautifully for the glory of the Lord.

I did not, of course, realise at the time of my marriage in 1958 that I was being wed to a man who would turn out to be a spiritual whirlwind for Jesus and be so much used by Him. Trevor became an itinerant evangelist in September 1970 and, from that time, I had to learn what it means to 'live by faith' with no fixed, secure income.

Eventually Trevor felt that I was called to minister alongside him for Jesus. Since that time I have been involved in a ministry of healing with Trevor. This has blessed people beyond my wildest dreams, for I have always felt myself to be a very ordinary woman, even though married to an extraordinary man. In all this I had before me, not the calling to some remarkable ministry, but the fact that I had been called to be a wife.

Everything else which you read in the following pages follows from that one absolutely sure Christian vocation which I have known from my earliest years—that God called me to the highest calling a woman can know, to be a wife and mother. It is by His grace alone that I have fulfilled this purpose in which I have found, despite many trials, such rich joy and fulfilment. If I ever had to live my life over again, I would make just the same choices. I would want it no other way.

1: 'I'm Going to Marry a Parson'

I was one of six young girls who were sitting around the old water pump in the centre of the village of Barnack, Lincolnshire, on a lovely hot summer's day. We were playing a children's game in which we were using our imagination to describe what sort of man we would one day marry,

'I want to marry a policeman!' exclaimed one of my friends, her eyes bright with excitement.

'And I want to marry a doctor,' added another, nearly breathless with joy.

'What about you, Anne?' they said in chorus. I had no hesitation in replying. 'I'm going to marry a parson!'

Many events had already influenced my young mind to the belief that a Church of England minister was the ideal choice.

From being a baby-in-arms I had been plagued with acute and chronic bronchitis, which threatened to take away my young life. We lived in a small agricultural worker's house in the village, my father being employed in the humble but, in many ways, beautiful work of a shepherd. I was the first-born of eight children who were cared for by very loving and hard-working parents.

I was not the only one of their children causing them anxiety about health, because they were soon to lose my brother Arthur, through an incurable complaint. My condition caused them not only emotional anxiety, but also many hours of lost sleep as they watched over me lying in a bed beside the fire, hacking away with my terrible cough night after night. The local doctor could do little to alleviate my distress but forecast that if I could be kept alive to the age of twelve, then the illness would never trouble me again. It was mainly through my parents' tender care and prayers, also because God wanted it so, that I lived through those years and, thankfully, I have never suffered with the disease since.

It was during this time when my brother and I were sick that I formed my childhood image of parsons as the most marvellous people in the world. The Reverend Nesbitt, our local Vicar, lived in a huge house nearby in our small but beautiful village. As he crossed the road to the parish church every morning to say prayers, I would stand up on my bed, from which vantage point I was just tall enough to look out through the window to the church over the road. I knew the exact time he would cross, for he never varied the hour. Eagerly I would wave my hand to him and shout 'Hello', in as loud a voice as my croaking throat would let me; and the gracious man never failed to turn round and return my greeting.

It wasn't only a distant contact I had with him. Regularly, at least once every week, he would knock on the door and visit my mother and encourage her with kindly words as she sought to look after her increasingly large family. I loved that man, and the collar around his neck spoke to my young heart of God, Someone up above the bright blue sky, who loved little children like me.

I suppose, looking back, I have had 'religious' inclinations for as long as I can remember, although my parents were not regular church-goers. They attended such festivals as Christmas, Easter and Harvest Thanksgiving and in their way, they certainly knew and loved God. I can still remember the times my father would take me on his knee and sing songs of faith to my heart. One which has lived with me over the years goes something like this.

A little lamb went straying
Among the hills one day,

Leaving its faithful shepherd
Because it loved to stray;
And while the sun shone brightly,
It knew no thought of fear;
For flowers around were blooming,
And balmy was the air.

But ah! the faithful shepherd
Soon missed the little thing,
And onward went to seek it,
Safe home again to bring.
He sought on hill, on valley,
And called it by its name;
He sought, nor ceased his seeking,
Until he found his lamb.

Albert Midlane

My parents also told us bible stories. In this way they gave us their own sort of religious education, which may not have been from a teacher's manual but certainly came from the heart. I can't really think of a time when, in however vague a way, I didn't know and love the God personified for me by the Reverend Nesbitt and my parents' example.

My parents' Bible teaching and the informal worship of our home were not the only sources of spiritual nurture which made such a life-long impression on me. There were also times when I was allowed out of doors, not only to play with my friends, but just to go walking by myself. I didn't have to walk far, because I loved going into the Church itself. Its door brings back many memories, for it is unchanged even today. It is very heavy with a stiff iron handle to turn, but by using all my strength, I would manage to push it open and sit inside the building. My eyes always went in one direction—towards a Crucifix. I would sit and gaze at it for long periods of time. I saw Jesus hanging there and even then, in my little child's mind, I knew that He wasn't on the Cross but was alive in some way and that I could know Him.

The village school was 'Church-aided', and the Vicar came in regularly to teach us the Church's Catechism. In those days, the value of committing passages of Scripture to memory had not been squashed by modern educational theories, and we children were asked to learn by heart the whole Catechism. I remember especially the words:

Question: Who made me?
Answer: God made me.
Question: Why did God make you?
Answer: God made me that I might know and love and serve Him here on earth and to live with Him for ever in Heaven.

These sentences have always had a profound effect upon my knowing who I am and why, ultimately, I am here living in this world.

A sad but vivid impression was made upon my mind by the passing of my younger brother Arthur. I was actually in the room when he died. It's rarely, I suppose, that a child of eight witnesses the death of a loved one. His passing, however, was remarkable. His beautiful face became even more angelic, as he looked up into a corner of the room and held out his arms, as if seeing some invisible Presence. He then turned and said, 'No, I want my Mammy,' as if reluctant to go away on an unknown journey. The next minute I saw him lying peaceful but still upon the bed.

Mr Nesbitt was soon on the scene. 'I have a special place reserved for little Arthur,' he said. 'It is a beautiful place in my churchyard.' His kindness and love seemed to bring peace to our grief-stricken home.

This, then, was the atmosphere in which I grew to adolescence, a home where both mother and father had to work long hard hours to provide the basic essentials for their children, where loving care was always known, where many hymns were sung and prayers said. Eventually I left school at the age of fourteen and began to earn my own living. Soon, because our house was rather small I chose to go into residential work, in our local boarding school.

They were happy days, and my childhood was full of rich, wholesome memories. Although times were difficult and the days hard, I grew up knowing how to feel and how to express love. Unknown to me, the foundation for my future life had been laid by my Saviour, who I now realise had known me from my mother's womb. Before my vision stood the tall, austere, strong but kindly Reverend Nesbitt, wearing his clerical collar, symbolising all I knew of God, preparing me in part for the day when I would marry a parson.

2: 'One shall be Taken'

By the time I had reached fourteen years of age the Second World War was over. The tragic events in Europe and the Far East hadn't much disturbed the tranquility of the Lincolnshire countryside. We had some prisoners-of-war working in the fields, to whom my parents were generous with what food we had to spare. A single large bomb was dropped nearby by a German aircraft fleeing from British aeroplanes and the crater was a source of wonder to the young people of the area.

By this time I had come to know two older Christian couples. The men, Mr Palmer and Mr Fred Shilcock, were agricultural workers and by human standards they were very ordinary and even unlearned men. But they were faithful Methodist local preachers, single-hearted and utterly dedicated to Jesus. They walked or cycled many miles nearly every Sunday to fulfil preaching engagements in the tiny Methodist sanctuaries scattered around our rural area.

I am sure that my deep friendship with these wonderful people was also part of God's preparation for me to become a wife to a wholehearted Christian minister. Even the Probationary Methodist Minister in the circuit, the Rev. George Sales, seemed to sense that the Lord had His hand upon me in a special way. I sometimes used to cycle with him to his appointments and we covered many miles talking about Jesus.

By this time I was becoming more and more a Methodist, although the deep impression made upon my young mind by Mr Nesbitt and the Barnack Church remained in my thoughts.

'Come and spend the day with us' was the frequent warm invitation of my new friends. They seemed to look upon me as a daughter, and they had an ever open door for me. I saw several things in the lives of these devoted Christian couples which made a lasting impression. Firstly, I saw the depth of the relationship which devoutly Christian men and their wives could have together as they shared the love of the Lord. Further, I began to realise that ordinary people could know Jesus in a very vivid and personal way and I saw the wonderful effect of such a relationship with Jesus on the whole of their lives. How well I remember Mr Palmer standing in the pulpit preaching fervently to just a handful of people, sounding, to use his favourite phrase, 'as Saint Paul of Old'!

Christian men and women, I am sure, should always have their hearts and homes open to children and young people who are receptive to the message of Jesus. Mr Nesbitt, for instance, faithfully carried out his work in the homes of his village, and died without ever knowing the profound effect he had on a little girl who would one day be the wife of an international evangelist. The Palmers and the Shilcocks taught me so much about Christian life, just by being what they were. They had the joy also of seeing me converted.

It was one of those 'accidents' which are arranged by God, which saw me in the small Methodist Church in the nearby village of Ketton one Sunday evening, waiting for Mr Shilcock to appear through the door to deliver one of his Bible-based messages. However, to my amazement not he but a young man emerged from the vestry. His name was announced as Ronald Hayward, who was studying at All Nations' Bible College for missionary work with the Japan Evangelistic Band.

That night he preached boldly about the Lord's Second Coming, especially expounding the text that on the Day of Judgment there would be two women working in the fields and, to quote the words of Jesus, 'one would be taken and the other left'. He stated that only those would be with the Lord in heaven who had 'confessed Him before men', having accepted Him as their personal saviour.

I realised that I had never done this and was swept with a sense of horror that I would be amongst those who would be left to endure life apart from God, in hell. Thankfully, he didn't stop there but asked any who hadn't accepted Jesus to raise their hands. An awful hush fell upon the small gathering as he awaited a response. A battle went on within me between desire and embarrassment, and the Holy Spirit won! Slowly but surely I raised my hand. 'I want to be with you, Lord,' I implored in my heart. Then there was peace, followed by excitement, I had become a real Christian in a moment of time, just like Mr and Mrs Palmer and Mr and Mrs Shilcock.

The young man wisely took my name and address and began to correspond with me on matters relating to the Christian faith. He was faithful in doing this for many years. O that all evangelists were like him! He is to this day an evangelist in Japan working for the Japan Evangelistic Band.

Events seemed to follow upon each other very rapidly from that time. I became a Sunday School teacher at Ketton Methodist Church, under the guidance of a Mrs Johnson, who is still remembered in the locality. Two other dear Christian people, seeing my fervour for our Lord, offered to pay for me to go for a week to a hotel called Hildenborough Hall in the South of England for a Christian holiday, where Christian teaching was given as part of the stay. Once again the influence upon me was incalculable as I learned how to study the Bible in depth. However, my going there led to my first experience of the cost of Christian discipleship.

In my early teens, I had become, it seems, attractive to young men and, at the time of going to Hildenborough Hall, I had had a year's frienship with a very nice-looking young man named John, who was four yars my senior. I suppose, considering my age, our friendship was rather serious. However, a division had emerged between us as John was reluctant to come to Church with me. I realised that we could not share what had become the deepest part of my young life: my relationship with Jesus. My visit to Hildenborough and my deepened consecration had made a decision inevitable.

'John,' I said on my return, 'I don't really think our friendship can continue as before.'

'Why?' he enquired full of alarm, propping up his new motorcycle against the kerb.

'Well,' I explained, 'you have never wronged me in any way, and you are a very nice person, but I just cannot have a deep friendship with a person who doesn't love Jesus.'

He tried hard, even coming to Church with me on one occasion. However, we both realised that the split between us was widening. I was very fond of him and it was all very hard, but there could be no competitor to Jesus. It was when we were arguing on a street corner that he said, 'If I can't take my motorcycle to heaven then I don't want to go!'

With an aching heart I replied, 'Sorry, John, it's no use. It will never work.' Within moments he was riding his motorcycle away up the hill. I was being called to be a wife, but had already learned the meaning of Paul's words: 'You cannot be unequally yoked with unbelievers.'

My friendship with John, who is now happily married, had a strange sequel. I introduced my mother to his brother Len during the time our friendship. Later, when my father, who was twenty years older then my mother, went to be with the Lord, Len and my mother met up again and were eventually married. He is a dear and beloved step-father.

Of course, my conversion experience was not fully understood by my parents at that time, but they always encouraged me in my Church-going and Christian friendships. I learnt far more words of wisdom from them than I can ever relate. They were also thrilled when I announced that as a result of my Christian experience I felt called to be a nurse. However, I was still too young to take up my training and so I went to be a general help on the staff of Cliff College, an evangelical establishment set amongst the hills of Derbyshire. The young men there were training to be evangelists. It was here, at a youth camp which I attended later from the hospital where I was training, that I met my husband Trevor.

3: 'Through Hidden Dangers, Toils and Deaths'

By the time I met Trevor I was twenty-two years of age and had been nursing at Rampton Psychiatric Hospital for three years. I had arrived there as a very raw recruit with no previous experience of nursing. I found it to be almost as much a prison as a hospital, because all the ward doors were locked and there were even punishment blocks for inmates who had misbehaved. It was a place for people with serious mental illness, and some of them had records of violence. It was for this reason that the staff were paid more than general nurses. It was considered as danger money!

The facilities for nurses were very comfortable and all our needs were well catered for in every way, with lovely rooms in which to relax and excellent recreational facilities. There was a hospital Church which was staffed by a Church of England chaplain.

To my surprise and consternation, however, I soon discovered that among the whole nursing staff I was the only evangelical Christian, with a real experience of the Risen Christ. I found that the Church of England offered me little or no spiritual support and I soon began to feel different from the rest off the staff; in fact, I began to wonder if I was odd! I found I could not join in many of the dancing and other parties in the staff recreational club as there was nothing of Jesus in them and much of what happened seemed to be in direct opposition to my Christian faith. I made no secret of my love for Jesus and my deep commitment to Him in my conversations with other nurses, with patients, with doctors and my superiors, the Ward

Sisters. Soon I found that I was being accused of being negative, though not critical, in attitude to much that went on in the nurses' off-duty time. I also reacted in my spirit to what I regarded as the sometimes harsh treatment of patients, which staff assured me was only being administered to control them, or for their good.

On the surface then, life for me at Rampton Hospital could have been very unhappy, but that was far from the case. I regard my time there as three very happy years and have since, in times of stress, even wished that I was back there with those patients!

I found that, despite the openness of my Christian faith, I made lots of friends amongst the staff, who seemed to respect and even like me as a person. My witness to them was no rehearsed speech or the 'giving of my testimony', neither did I feel superior to them in any way. My Christian conversation seemed to flow naturally from my lips as well as from my life. I well rememeber one nurse, to whom I had drawn particularly close, saying that she wished beyond all else that she had my Christian faith and knew my beloved Lord. I helped her as best I could, and was privileged to lead her into a knowledge of Jesus as Saviour.

Once again the Lord's providential care was over me in that He gave me more than one Christian home in the locality where I could go for Christian fellowship when I was off duty. All these came from my attendance at evangelical Churches in the neighbouring town of Retford. I can well remember one such occasion when I dared to go into the local Brethren Assembly. As I sat there a lady came over to me and asked if I was 'saved'. 'Yes,' I said, 'I know Jesus as my own personal Saviour.' She then invited me to her home and I met her family and often visited them. Another contact came on a bus when I began to talk about the Lord to a lady sitting next to me, who turned out to be a member of the Salvation Army. Yet another door was opened to me and I was introduced to yet another Christian young man!

My deepest friendship and fellowship, however, was with

one of the senior doctors at the hospital, Dr Robert Porter, and with his dear wife Joan. Once again , I was welcomed into their home at any time and I saw there perhaps the most beautiful Christian relationship between husband and wife, parents and children that I have ever known. It was a model Christian home. Once again I had found a source of rich spiritual strength and encouragement which helped me in my ongoing Christian life and service, in what was generally a non-Christian environment.

Dr Porter had his own small independent Church fellowship, which met in a hut on the hospital campus. This was a real means of blessing. He maintained it himself, often both playing the organ and preaching. So often his message was: 'Is your heart right with God? Washed in the crimson flood? Cleansed and made holy, humble and lowly, right in the sight of God?' It was a place from which a real evangelical challenge rang out. I could confidently take contacts there knowing they would be introduced to the living Jesus. Dr Porter himself never compromised his Christian convictions and was a highly respected member of the medical profession throughout the hospital.

Patients were not allowed to go to the doctor's chapel but I found ample opportunity to talk to them about Jesus on the wards. Sometimes I would read stories about Him to patients whose mentality was that of young children and, in the way Jesus said, they accepted Him with childlike faith. Patients often looked forward eagerly to my turns on duty. It was a rich rewarding time.

I do thank God, however, for at least four occasions when He probably saved me from being raped or even murdered. One involved a young man who was an extremely good-looking nurse, much admired by all the young women on the staff. He was not a Christian, but he asked me out for a date. I suppose I was somewhat flattered and agreed to go. I was unwise enough to allow him to take me into a dark field where he began to make advances towards me. It soon became obvious that his intentions were to go 'the whole way' and I began to panic as he wouldn't take 'no' for an answer. The situation became very frightening and I prayed, 'O Lord, deliver me.' I found myself giving my testimony and even asking him if he wanted to be saved. He fled! I returned to my room minus my belt and in a dishevelled and shocked state. I learned my lesson from this and never again went out with someone who wasn't a Christian!

Another threatening occasion occurred when I was on night duty. As usual I went round each bed and isolation room on a tour of inspection to see if all the patients were asleep. I peered through the inspection block at Rosemary, one of my favourite patients, who had often heard me tell the stories of Jesus. She was awake looking pale and ill. I knew her well and felt no danger as I unlocked the door and went in to take her temperature. The hospital rules stating that no nurses should visit a patient alone were far from my thoughts. Had I been more experienced I would have known that she was 'unsettled' rather than physically ill. Suddenly she leapt out of bed and pushed me hard back against the door. By God's grace I managed to escape her clutches and lock the door once again. Of course I had to report the incident and received a gentle but firm rebuke from the night-sister.

I was deeply moved, however, the next morning when Rosemary cried out in a heartbroken voice, 'I'm sorry, Nurse Steele, I didn't mean to hurt you. You're the last person in the world I would hurt.' Tears ran down her cheeks, all was forgiven!

The two other incidents when God's providential care was obvious were in connection with car rides. There was thought to be no danger in those days for young women 'thumbing lifts' and nurses then, as now, were always underpaid and short of money. My parents' home, which I loved to visit on every possible occasion, was about eighty miles away on a major road. Naturally, therefore, I was sometimes to be seen waiting on that road hoping some driver would give me a lift home.

I remember one very obliging man who was driving his fish van to the town of Stamford, not far from my home. I unhesitatingly accepted his offer. I was naive and credited everybody with my own pure motives. It was getting late in the day and we had a pleasant conversation until he turned off the main road into a deserted side road which was not in the right direction at all.

'What do you think you are doing?' I asked him, in real fear, as he made amorous advances towards me. It was then that the Lord came to my aid.

'Do you want a cigarette?' he asked, obviously trying to gain my favour.

'I don't smoke,' I replied.

'Do you dance?' he asked.

'No!' I replied.

'What do you do then?' he said. 'Nurses are not known to be as slow as you are.'

'I'm a Christian,' I announced, putting all my trust in the Name of Jesus.

To my relief he started up his engine and drove me to Stamford in silence. As I got out of his van he said, 'You know, you're a lucky girl. Many men would have taken advantage of you.'

'Not all men are like you,' I retorted. 'Most are honourable.'

However, that was my last hitch-hiking expedition. I later thanked God again as He delivered me from a car driver in Stamford Town, who, with his companion, tried to lure me into a car and, but for passers-by, might have dragged me in.

Despite such episodes, my time at Rampton holds many happy memories for me. I learned so much more about the ways of our wonderful Lord, and felt even more than before His providential care over me as I served Him as a nurse. I suppose it would have been easy for me to backslide in that environment where so many worldly pleasures and attractive young men sought my attention. However, the Lord never forsakes those who truly trust in Him, and honours those who maintain an uncompromising witness to Him. He opens many doors when we are friendly and do not stand in judgment or remain aloof from those who have not discovered the privilege of knowing Him.

When all thy mercies, O my God,
My rising soul surveys,
Transported with the view, I'm lost
In wonder, love and praise.

When in the slippery paths of youth
With heedless steps I ran,
Thine arm, unseen, conveyed me safe,
And led me up to man.

Through hidden dangers, toils and deaths,
It gently cleared my way;
And through the pleasing snares of vice,
More to be feared than they.

Joseph Addison

God was keeping me safe for the tremendous days of service that lay ahead for me, with Trevor.

4: 'And the Two shall be One flesh'

Cliff College in Derbyshire was by far my favourite place for my holidays. I would never miss the Conventions at Whitsuntide and August, when the grounds were packed with young people of my age, who had gathered to praise the Lord and listen to famous speakers. Honoured adult guests stayed in the College itself, whilst the students gave up their rooms for them and slept in tents with other young men out in the extensive grounds. We girls had somewhat better facilites in bunk beds in pre-fabricated huts. We shared large communal meals and few people ever complained as above all the discomforts was an atmosphere of joy, love and expectancy. I met all my friends there twice a year, and often when I left had made a promise to correspond with yet another Christian young man. I was fortunate, I felt, in having so many friends of both sexes.

Although I had reached the age of twenty-one without any serious involvement with a young man, I was never anxious because I had a deep sense that, if I kept faithful to Him, my heavenly Father would one day clearly indicate the person of His choice whom I would marry. I would recognise him. He would be tall, have a lively mind and he would be a 'Jesus man.'

It happened one day as I was sitting cleaning the camp cutlery with one of my friends. We had stayed on after the close of the Convention to help the students tidy everything away for next year. I had had a most enjoyable week and was sitting at the entrance to the large communal dining hall. Suddenly, as I was talking to my friend, almost from 'out of the blue' he stood there—a student I had never seen before. The Lord had told me that 'my man' of his choice would be tall, have a good mind and love Him dearly. These thoughts, however, were not even in my mind as I gazed up at the tall form of a young man who seemed to take my breath away. He was tall, but not in any way outstanding to look at. He was wearing a brown-coloured working suit, which was much too short for him, because he had been doing manual work. When he smiled I noticed he was missing a tooth at the front and his hair was all over the place. He had merely paused to speak to my friend, whom he obviously knew, before entering the tea hall. He greeted me with a few courteous words, and in a matter of moments went on his way.

'Who was that?' I gasped to my friend Enid. I was excited because I had that strange inner feeeling, which is indescribable to those who haven't had it, that I had met my future husband.

'He's called Trevor Dearing,' explained Enid. 'He's one of the students who knows my boyfriend Ivor. I can introduce him to you, if you want.'

'Please do that,' I urged. 'I do want to know him.'

I felt then that I should never want to go out with any other young man. Sure enough, Enid did the introductions! I went to bed that night so excited I could hardly sleep. I was in one of the evangelists' houses, the camp having been packed away.

The next morning I was awakened by the sound of small pebbles being thrown at the window. Dreamily I got out of bed, and there was Trevor!

'Hey!' he shouted. 'It's time you were up. There's work to do. I'll meet you at breakfast.' I dashed away to get ready for a very important meal.

We chatted away at the meal, side-by-side. He happened to see a photograph I had recently had taken in my nurse's uniform and which I kept in my Bible, and seemed impressed. It didn't take more than a few minutes of conversation for me to realise how deeply he was committed to Christ and what an intelligent, clear-thinking young man he was.

'What time is your train home?' he enquired.

I told him it was very soon but that I could get a later one.

'Do that,' he said, 'then we can walk up Calver Sough.'

This was the famous lovers' walk that led to the brow of some high rocks overlooking the college. I needed no persuading!

As we walked together on a lovely summer's day, he explained to me that he was offering himself for the ministry of the Methodist Church and hoped to be accepted for training that year. My childhood words 'I'm going to marry a parson' rang in my memory.

Before we were half-way up the steep rise he had taken my hand. I felt every bird was singing. We reached the top and sat down to rest. There we talked, holding each other in an embrace I never wanted to end. Eventually, however, that train had to be caught. He came to Sheffield Railway Station and we waved each other a temporary 'good-bye'.

'Lord,' I prayed, 'let your will be done quickly!'

Trevor and I corresponded regularly during the next few months. He told me that before going into Methodist Theological College he was going to serve a year as a Methodist Lay Pastor in country Churches in Norfolk. Of course, neither of us possessed a car and we were very short of money, I as a student nurse and he as a trainee minister. Could I go a whole year without seeing him? The answer seemed to come in an advertisement for a nurse in an isolation hospital in Holt, Norfolk.

'Lord, let your will be done,' I gasped once again—and I got the job not many miles from where Trevor would be working. He was delighted and later said my being there had helped him a great deal in what could otherwise have been a very lonely year.

Our happiness was marred, however, by a factor which was completely out of our control. At that time Methodist Ministers were not allowed to be married until they had completed their three years' studies in college and a further three as trainee ministers. We were very much in love and faced with a seven-year wait before we could marry. That meant Trevor would be twenty-eight and I would be twenty-nine. A physical relationship before we were married was, of course, unthinkable to both of us. What could we do? I knew I had to urge Trevor to pursue his course to the ministry. He explained to me that he hoped that he wouldn't meet his wife-to-be for at least another three years!

The whole situation put us under a great deal of emotional stress, to such an extent that Trevor thought at one stage that he would have to say a heart-broken farewell to release me. This, despite the strain, was in no way what we wanted and after much prayer, we became engaged to be married.

The stress, however, was none the less when Trevor entered Wesley Theological College, Leeds. I moved again, this time to a geriatric hospital, St George's at Rothwell, near Leeds. Trevor and I were then able to meet often. He seemed to be having a particularly difficult time, however, and was anxious, sometimes moody and even angry at the whole system. Yet I knew God had shown me that Trevor and I were born to marry each other. I knew he loved me deeply—that was his trouble!

The answer came! Suddenly the Methodist Church announced that its trainee ministers *could* marry as soon as they left college. We were 'over the moon' with delight. The Methodist Church had never experienced so many of its probationary ministers getting married in the same month!

Trevor left college at the age of twenty-four with a Bachelor of Divinity Degree, and I was twenty-five when, because of a traffic jam, I arrived at my wedding twenty minutes late. I stood beside Trevor at the Communion rail of the Barn Hill Methodist Church, Stamford, Lincolnshire, four miles away from the Parish Church of Barnack, and said, 'I will take this man to be my wedded husband; to have and to hold, for better or worse, richer or poorer, till death do us part.'

As we walked out of the church a lady from Norfolk where Trevor had ministered handed us an envelope containing £20. It was enough to enable us to have a week's honeymoon in the inexpensive but pleasant rooms of a hotel in Scarborough. We returned to our bed-sit home in Leeds. We looked at each other and realised that we had no money—but we had each other. God had called me to be a wife—a parson's wife!

5: 'For Better, for Worse'

Trevor continued his studies at Wesley College for a further year after we were married. We enjoyed our bed-sit because it was there that we had each other. We had to rely on my low pay as a nurse to pay the rent and provide all we needed. Then I became pregnant, with morning sickness and all other discomforts which come with this condition! We had planned to have a child because we knew that in a few months we would be moving into a fully-furnished Methodist Manse. I was still twenty-five years and we wanted to have our family while I was as young as possible. It was during this time that some dear Methodist friends kindly invited us to move into their home, an offer which we were in no position to refuse.

It was in 1958 that we moved to the Brighouse (West Yorkshire) Methodist Church, Trevor's first appointment wearing a clerical collar! I became quite enormous as the months went by and so we prepared for what the medical profession told us would be a large baby. On 11th September, having just scrubbed the bathroom and kitchen floors, I complained of pain in my back. Trevor quickly took me along to the doctor's surgery, and he decided to send me to the maternity hospital in case they were labour pains, although, being a month away from the anticipated delivery date, he said he doubted that they were.

I could hardly believe what happened next. Once I was in hospital the pains became worse and I was taken to the Labour Room. I had an agonising three hours before a baby girl came struggling into the world. I gasped with relief. To my amazement, however, the doctor told me not to give up as there was another child to be born! He said it was a 'breech' and after a time, during which I thought I would surely die, our second daughter announced her presence in the world! Trevor phoned the hospital the next morning.

'How's my wife?' he asked the nurse. 'She came in last night for observation.'

'Oh!' replied the nurse. 'We have a surprise for you.'

'The baby must have been born then,' Trevor enquired.

'More than that,' she said. 'You are the father of twins!'

'No!' gasped Trevor. 'I must repeat, my name is *Dearing*.'

'I heard the first time,' the nurse retorted. 'And you should be proud, you have twins.'

Trevor almost dropped the telephone with shock which, he said later, turned from disbelief to numbed surprise!

He came to see me as soon as possible, we laughed and embraced and congratulated ourselves, but the first item for discussion was which name we should choose for our surprise child, an unexpected gift from God! Ruth seemed to both of us to be a good choice.

I insisted on leaving hospital as soon as possible but had to leave the babies behind for further care. Together they had weighed over twelve pounds, but they were not feeding properly. Eventually we were able to bring Lyn (now called Rebecca) and Ruth home and the most hectic life imaginable began.

We were over a hundred miles from our nearest relatives. We had hardly been in Brighouse for more than a few days so we knew very few people. Trevor had three Churches to look after, much visiting to do, many business meetings to administer, and he had also to complete his compulsory and exacting post-collegiate studies. I had to keep a large house clean, prepare his meals, do an enormous amount of washing, and constantly be feeding two children who cried most of the day and all of the night, one disturbing the other! We both became very exhausted. Financially we were nearly destitute. One of Trevor's Churches delighted us by having a surprise 'baby shower' after the American pattern and we were well supplied with the twins' requirements for several months. Trevor was able to sell the pram and get a heavy coach-built one second-hand for the two babies. Everything had to be doubled! We were finding it so difficult to make ends meet that I often bought bacon bones for a few pence in order to boil them for a nourishing meal. I made a bacon pie with the bits of meat which fell off the bones.

Of course, we had no car and we both found the hills around Brighouse exhausting. Trevor had to cycle on all his visitation rounds and to services, which were often several miles away. I had an even more difficult task in pushing the heavy pram, laden with shopping, up the steep hill from the town centre to our home.

Life was very hard work. The Lord was providing our daily bread, though there was little in the way of luxury, but together we counted all things as His gift as we struggled on. As a wife I found that my calling was to work extremely hard in keeping my children well cared for and the home clean and comfortable for my very hard-working husband. I had to accept our poor situation and wear second-hand clothes at times, but tried in it all not to burden him or complain, but win through with the help of the Lord. Every day I said: 'I will lift up mine eyes unto the hills from whence cometh my help. My help cometh from the Lord, who made heaven and earth' (Psalm 121).

One of the ways He definitely helped was one morning when there was a knock at the door. I answered it to a woman I recognised as from Trevor's smallest Church at Clifton.

'I'm Sara,' she said. 'May I come in?'

She sat down in a room where a pile of ironing awaited my attention. She took in the entire situation with a knowing glance.

'Now,' she said, with some firmness, 'I'm an experienced domestic help for a doctor and another family and it just happens I have every Thursday morning free. I feel the Lord wants me here to help you.'

My embarrassment must have shown on my face, but she

went on, 'I know you will not be able to pay me so I will not be wanting any money. But, just so you can feel you are paying me and I can tell others who ask that you are, you just give me two shillings and sixpence.'

This we knew was her ingenious way of saving our pride. She came every Thursday morning as long as we were in Brighouse and often at other times as well. She was an angel in disguise.

Others too in the Churches were very kind to us in our need. We were often invited out to meals carrying our twins with us. Once, when Trevor had to have two weeks' break after collapsing with exhaustion, a family took care of the children for ten days whilst the Methodist Chairman of the District used some of his Discretionary Fund to send us away for a break.

We were less fortunate, however, in our dealings with the other 'officialdom' of Methodism. Things began to go wrong, for instance, in our dealings with the local Circuit Stewards who administered and controlled the local funds in relation to ministers and their houses. Twice I felt hurt over matters related to our home. One was in its decoration. We spent hours at their request choosing the colour for the exterior painting of our manse, only to find they had ignored our choice and painted it a horrible colour which they said would be 'more lasting'. They had it done while we were away from the house. On another occasion they put an old suite of furniture into our house, promising it would be re-upholstered. To our amazement, however, they went back on this promise telling us we had to 'make do'.

Being a wife to a parson was proving to be far from the glamorous picture I had had as a girl at the village water pump!

Trevor especially seemed to be beset by trials. He had gone into theological College as a keen, evangelical, Bible-believing Christian, having been trained as an evangelist at Cliff College. However, the theological training in Leeds was of a very different nature. Certainly I noticed a change in his outlook on the Bible and he seemed to be reacting from his Cliff College experience. This I discovered to be very common amongst students leaving 'Cliff' for training for the Methodist ministry. My own relatively simple faith in my Heavenly Father and my Saviour was still strong and I found myself hanging on to all I knew of Jesus. This, Trevor told me later, was an enormous help to him during his theological crises. Even after all these years, as I write, the faith I learned from the Palmers, Shilcocks, Porters and speakers at Cliff College is more firm than ever. I am grateful to God that Trevor found my grasp of the faith such a help at a time when his own evangelical faith was wavering.

He did, however, become very exhausted with all that was happening around his life and three factors eventually emerged which radically changed our lives. The first, small but important, was when the Circuit Stewards banned an effort by one of our churches to provide Trevor with a motorised bicycle to help him in his travels around the area. The second was the growing admiration he had for our local Vicar and his curates, for the depth of their spirituality and their sacramental and devotional lives. The final strain came as we were nearing the end of his time as a Probationary Minister at Brighouse. Trevor dearly wished to become the Minister of a Methodist Mission Church anywhere in the country so that, unlike in the Methodist circuit system, he could have only one Church building to be the centre of his ministry. This was the only Methodism Trevor had known since his dramatic conversion and miraculous healing in a Methodist Mission Church at the age of nineteen. now he wanted to return as a Minister to such a Church. After extensive enquiry he was told that he 'didn't know the right people' to secure such a post.

He was thoroughly disillusioned with Circuit Methodism and became drawn to the Church of England. The day of crisis I had anticipated eventually dawned. We sat at supper one evening and as I looked across at the strained face of my dear, tired husband who had worked his heart out in his Churches, for his family, and above all for His Lord, he said, 'Anne, will you go with me into the Church of England?'

I only wanted what he desired. I had been confirmed at twelve years of age and still pictured the Rev. Nesbitt going to church daily for Parish Prayers.

'If that's what you really want, darling,' I replied. 'Are you sure?'

He was sure, and within a short space of time had handed in his resignation as a Probationary Minister (he never was ordained in Methodism). We both loved Wesley and all he stood for, but hadn't he himself said, 'I live and die a member of the Church of England'?

Sadly, we thought, the local paper made his transfer of allegiance front-page news. Quickly we received a letter stating that Trevor's resignation had been accepted, apparently not very gracefully, and we were told we had to take our family and leave the manse without delay. We supported each other in those trying days. Trevor needed, I realised, a strong but gentle wife. I prayed I would be just that as we left in a removal van for Queen's Anglican Theological College in the city of Birmingham.

6: 'For Richer, For Poorer'

The transition from Methodism to the Church of England was not carried through without difficulty. The Bishop of Wakefield, who had promised to ordain Trevor, had asked him to be in residence at the Queen's Theological College in Birmingham in order, as he put it, 'to absorb the Anglican ethos'. Trevor's Bachelor of Divinity Degree enabled him to read for a Master of Arts at Birmingham University whilst the process of integration was going on. What it meant to me and our young family was, as the Americans would say, 'something else'.

Firstly, we had no home; secondly, we had no furniture; and thirdly, we had no money. The Vicar of Brighouse, the Rev. John Lister, promised that we could live in the Parish Church Hall but thankfully this was not necessary as, in direct answer to prayer, we were offered the use of an empty curate's house in Birmingham. However, the Vicar there required that we should pay rent in advance. We were penniless! We turned to every Charity we knew. The Bishop of Wakefield was very helpful not only in paying the bills the Methodist Church was now sending us for Trevor's past training (thankfully they eventually stopped sending them), but also in providing money for our removal and the initial rent for the house. He sent us money during what was to prove the most difficult financial year of our lives, whenever we reached rock bottom. We were also helped by the Church Times Train-a-Priest Fund.

However, we had also to help ourselves and so, in order to support Trevor in his training year, I had to leave my small family during the night in order to nurse, then look after them during the day, half asleep.

Furniture was our main problem when we set off to live in our new home. I can well remember that as I was travelling to the house with our two little children, first by train and then by bus (Trevor had gone in the small removal van), I stopped to buy some linoleum which was an odd size and was being sold cheaply. I decided to spend the last of my savings on it only to find to my dismay that bus conductors would not let me on the bus with it, saying it was too large. At last, after I had been refused several times, a conductor relented and allowed me to board his vehicle. It was thus that I struggled to the house with my family and the lino which I wasn't even sure would fit anywhere.

Our furniture would have been a laugh if it hadn't been so tragic. We had just one old carpet to put on the floor, besides the lino, so we walked on the floor boards, every step resounding through the small house. We had no curtains at the windows and undressed behind an old wardrobe door. Our dressing table consisted of five cases full of clothes placed on top of each other, covered with a cloth and with a mirror perched on the top. We had been given an old suite of furniture by the Vicar who had given us the wardrobe, so we had something to sit on which was a little more comfortable than the floor. The table off which we ate had been used as a bird table in the Vicar's garden which I scrubbed clean. We had an old-fashioned bed and the children had a cot each and that was it—the first home to call our own!

The house was very dirty as it hadn't been lived in for some time. Dirt, dust and grease were everywhere. We worked all day and into the night to get it clean. When we had finished we felt proud of our home and we joined in prayer to thank our Heavenly Father for His goodness! We had our daily bread and He supplied all our *needs.*

Trevor was, as usual, very hard-working and began to work as a 'nursing orderly' (nursing assistant) at a nearby psychiatric hospital, where he was reasonably paid and learned a great deal about counselling emotionally disturbed people. He did this in all his vacations from the College. Further hardship, however, was added by the fact that married students were not allowed to live outside the College during term time and so I was robbed of his support when I badly needed it.

A crisis came upon us in a most unexpected way during an Easter vacation. Trevor had been unable to secure a post at the hospital to earn money and, in the end, finished up doing accountancy work at a jewellery works in the City. He discovered on his arrival that the firm's books were in a terrible mess owing to the dishonesty of the previous accountant. In a very short time he had sorted everything out (he had once studied accountancy as a teenager) and trained another person for the task. The owner of the business was so impressed that he asked Trevor if he was really serious about being a parson or whether he wouldn't rather stay in a high salaried position, with the prospect of a directorship and eventual ownership of the business. Trevor arrived home on Friday evening for his meal very excited with the news.

'The Managing Director has given me until Sunday at 6 pm to decide,' he said. 'He will be phoning then for my decision. What do you think, Anne?'

We both looked around our poorly furnished, rented home and realised that it was if we were being offered the earth. We prayed, 'Lord, show us clearly your will.'

But we knew, before we prayed what God's will was, for Trevor had been called to full-time ministry in the Christian Church as surely as he breathed. He knew it and so did I. It was then that I realised that Trevor mught well fall for the temptation. He loved me and his children as much as any man could. He wanted the very best for us. He was unhappy with our impoverished state and with my tired eyes after another night on duty as a nurse. He was excited. He had, it seemed, been given a way of escape. I knew in those moments, more clearly than ever before, the role a wife had to fulfil, no matter what the cost.

'Trevor,' I pleaded, 'don't do it. For the love of God stay with those studies another year. With His help we *can* get through and I am with you all the way.'

We spoke of all Jesus had said about gaining the whole world and losing one's soul. We looked up all the verses about the cost of discipleship and for myself the cost of now being married to a parson.

Our home had always been a place of prayer. Sara had remarked on it more than once in her time with us. Even many years later, at our Silver Wedding celebrations she told everyone present of the sacred moments, even in the midst of harrowing domestic activity, that she had spent in prayer with us at our request. Never, however, had it been more important for us to hear the Master's voice than now.

Our first feelings were finally confirmed by the inner witness of our hearts at five-thirty on the Sunday. Trevor was ready when the phone rang at six to say to the firms's owner, 'I am grateful for your offer, but I know that all my life I must serve the Lord in a full-time capacity. I must be a clergyman.' My heart rejoiced. I had sustained and supported Trevor in his own 'wilderness experience' of decision about the direction his life had to go.

The 'boss' was impressed by Trevor's sincerity and gave him a farewell present of six solid silver serviette rings, which still today remind us of what was perhaps the most critical weekend in our spiritual pilgrimage together. I had been called to be a parson's wife—for better or worse, for richer or poorer and, though it was 'for poorer', a parson's wife I would be.

7: Being a Parson's Wife

Our circumstances could only get better when Trevor finished his year at the Church of England Theological College. The following years saw us in the Parishes of Todmorden (Lancs.), Silkstone and Northowram, Halifax (West Yorkshire), and Harlow (Essex). We were helped in our removal from Birmingham to Todmorden by the Poor Clergy Relief Corporation, who also sent us gifts of clothes for ourselves and the children for two consecutive years. Trevor's Vicar, however, allowed him to do part-time teaching and to finish his Master of Arts Degree, whilst still working hard as a Curate. Trevor continued some teaching in colleges after he became Vicar of Silkstone and so, slowly but surely, our financial burden was lifted.

In the meantime, I gave birth to two more children, Rachael, a delightful little girl, when we lived at Silkstone, and Philip, who came upon us by surprise while Trevor was Vicar of Northowram. All this meant that we lived extremely busy lives. This in itself was a source of stress as on many days Trevor and I only seemed to see each other for hurried meals and both of us dropped into bed very tired.

Trevor's ministry was traditional 'middle of the road' Anglican, although his 'learning' used to come across a lot in his sermons. He was an assiduous visitor and youth worker and an energetic Vicar. He seemed, even in those days, to draw a lot of attention from the local press in some of his adventures and utterances, and was always well-known in the locality as one who uncompromisingly spoke his mind.

Yet he often used to express to me how dissatisfied he was

with his ministry. He numbered only two genuine conversion experiences amongst his hearers. He seemed to get involved in all sorts of extra-clerical activities such as organising garden fetes, model railway exhibitions, pantomime productions and so on. He often used to say that he was bored with his own services! Whenever he tried to introduce anything from his evangelical days at Cliff College he was firmly told by Church leaders, 'We are Anglican and Anglican we remain.' Once we tried to arrange for a coach-load of people to attend Billy Graham rallies and a mission in Leeds, only to meet with apathy or even antagonism on the part of our people.

I was now experiencing the reality of what it meant to be married to the man I loved—what it meant to be a parson's wife in *today's* world. It was certainly very different from my idyllic picture of the small village Church in Barnack, with the Rev. Nesbitt caring for his small flock, supported obviously by a large private income. He had even had servants in his house and his wife had been more like a 'lady of the manor'. His daughter had attended a private school and had often been addressed with the title 'Miss'.

When my children were very young our parishioners had been understanding enough to realise that my hands were full with caring for my family. However, as the children grew a little older, I realised that I was expected to be a sort of leader amongst the ladies in the Church, a public speaker, an enrolling member of the Mother's Union and so on. All this was in addition to the constant answering of the telephone and dealing with messages and callers at the Vicarage door when Trevor was out. I was expected also to see that my children were at Church and Sunday School (a pressure against which vicarage children frequently react later in life). I had to entertain visitors on many occasions and arrange cheese and wine parties to raise money for parish funds. The list of jobs was endless.

Trevor tried to shelter me and the home in which we lived as much as possible, but as his office was in the house it was difficult for him to do. So I was frequently, for instance, leaving the children in the bath tub to dash downstairs to answer the door, or burning the potatoes on the hot-plate because I couldn't get away from the telephone! What a 'hurly-burly' life it was... being married to a parson! Trevor was good in keeping his day-off to be with the children and me and he did his best to give us his attention at other times. But there was always the car (which we now owned) to clean, or the garden to tidy. Really, only those who have lived vicarage life in busy parishes, with a very conscientious parson as a husband, can fully appreciate what it is like, and how a husband and wife can grow apart from each other without realising it. However, I had been called to be a wife and now, as a parson's wife, I stuck to my task to the best of my ability.

I would perhaps have found the parochial duties of a parson's wife easier had I not been by nature a very shy person. Throughout my life, I have always found it hard to cope under pressure from others, so that tasks which I might cope with quite happily if left alone became traumatic events. So life was becoming more and more intolerable as I felt parishioners pushing me into roles which it was not my nature to fill. At the same time I felt that if I failed to fulfil the expectations of notable women in the parish, I was letting Trevor down and putting him in a difficult position when he was asked 'Will your wife take it on?'

The position was particularly difficult if I was following a Vicar's wife who had been very capable at organising parish functions, leading the women and speaking at public engagements. This was so at St. Matthew's, Northowram, where I began to feel very inadequate. A Vicar's wife, it seemed to me now, must be a special calling in the Church, much more than simply being married to a man who happened to be a Vicar. At Northowram, too, there were some likeable but very strong and capable women. God bless them! They didn't mean to do it, but just by being themselves they made me feel inadequate—not as a wife, but as a *parson's* wife.

Other things were not going too well for us either. The

vicarage was a lovely house but needed a lot of money to heat it. It was also in bad need of decoration. I set about the task of wallpapering and painting. Trevor helped when he could, as did my brother-in-law when he visited. When it came to the large hall and stairway, however, we gave up. It needed professional attention with proper ladders and so on. We asked the Parochial Church Council for help, fully expecting they would agree without hesitation. However, they asked Trevor to leave the meeting whilst they discussed the matter. From our vicarage we could see the lights on and knew that the meeting was going on until past midnight.

The next morning the Churchwarden came around to say that they had decided to pay half the amount. We were shattered! It took our last penny to find the remainder.

The same decision was reached about Trevor's rapidly rising postage and travel expenses at another midnight session. We were beginning to feel somewhat hurt and confused!

The Church had some lovely people as members, but was, in the main, as much a social as a worshipping centre. It did have a few deeply devotional people and Trevor, who was now re-discovering his evangelical zeal through fellowship with some Bible-believing clergy, was able to lead at least one young married woman into a living relationship with the Lord. She is still a licensed lady-worker in the parish doing a wonderful work for Jesus.

However, our other efforts at deepening the spirituality of the members met with little success. We tried Bible Studies, Prayer Meetings and Discussion Groups at the vicarage but they were abysmally attended, especially in contrast to the folk who flocked to the house for cheese and wine evenings or the Church hall for the model-railway exhibition. Despite much pleasantness and some happy memories, it all seemed very disconcerting.

It was at this time that Trevor and I met up with the Rev. and Mrs John Bradbury in a Halifax parish. We became very friendly with them and noted their radiant faces, beautiful ministry and love for Jesus. They talked now and then about what they called 'the baptism of the Holy Spirit' and the joy of speaking with tongues. We didn't really understand what it was all about but they were sowing seeds which would soon bear fruit as Trevor and I, feeling disillusioned with being a parson and a parson's wife, set off for an appointment in Harlow, Essex, where he was to be Head of Religious Education at a large comprehensive school and also a part-time Curate in the evangelical Town Centre parish.

8: A Changed Husband

Harlow offered me no respite from the pressures in my life. The situation had in fact become so acute that I had reached a 'rock bottom' condition in Halifax and had had to spend two weeks in hospital as a result of a breakdown. The children were still young but I undertook some part-time employment. Trevor's new sphere of work meant however, that for the first time since our marriage we were buying our own home. It was no longer like being a refugee in Church property. I had my own home to take pride in and I devoted my energies to making it as nice as possible. It felt good. The house was of a size which was manageable in every way. Trevor was now working fixed hours both as a teacher and curate. Now, like other wives, I would have him at home most evenings, at the weekends and for holidays. I felt at last that I was a wife and mother in a way that God intended, a way that made sense. It seemed at last that the most unfulfilled part of me was being met, that I was by nature and calling a *homemaker*!

We made our average-sized house and garden as beautiful as we could. At the same time Trevor was enjoying being on the staff of a large evangelical parish, with the deep fellowship that it brought, which he so much needed. As I sat in Church hearing him preaching the Gospel, I reflected on the days in Silkstone and Halifax when he had seemed so lost spiritually, days when I had hung on to my evangelical faith and had had to use every method at my disposal to get him along to missions held by the Cliff College students or by Eric Hutchings and Billy Graham. I had never given up and it was I who had made all the initial contacts with evangelical clergymen in our area, in order to keep Trevor's faith alive. Now I knew that my prayers for Trevor had been answered. He was 'at home' again in the warm Christian fellowship not only of the team of ministers, but also of the deeply committed Christians of the Church of St. Paul, Harlow. Events however, were soon to take place which would test my faith and lead us into uncharted seas.

My father, had died whilst we were at Silkstone, actually in our home. I had been extremely close to him, and although he was over seventy years of age, his passing caused me deep sorrow. However, the news which broke upon us in Harlow, that my only brother, at thirty years of age, was suffering from cancer, was devastating. No one at St. Paul's, Harlow, not even Trevor, seemed to be able to offer me the help for which I was looking. A new spiritual dimension, however, began to be opened up when I was sharing my desperate concern with a neighbouring vicar, the Rev. John Tyndale-Biscoe who, with his wife Margie, had been invited to our home for an evening of fellowship.

'Have you ever heard of the evangelist called Peter Scothern?' John enquired. When I replied that I had not, he went on, 'I had arthritis in my neck and I went to him for prayer and all the pain has gone.'

Immediately I became very interested. 'Where can I meet up with him?' I asked.

'Well, I do know that he visits a small Pentecostal Church near Welwyn Garden City,' John said, 'I will see if I can find out further details.'

John was true to his word and I soon knew of an evening when this healing evangelist would be taking a meeting at the Church. Trevor had remained very quiet about the whole subject but as the evening drew nearer, he began to voice his opposition to my venture.

'I have never liked Pentecostal Churches,' he said emphatically. 'They are places for the emotionally unstable and the theologically unsound. It's all nothing but sheer emotionalism and I'm sorry, but I wouldn't darken the doors of the place!' He went on to say that he was very opposed to my going that he wouldn't even take me there in the car and, as I didn't drive, I would have to go the thirty miles on the bus. However, I was determined to seek out any possible help for my brother and so, leaving Trevor behind to look after the children, I set out on my way.

The church building was so small I almost missed it. However, eventually I arrived, somewhat late, and took my seat among about sixty people who were singing choruses to praise the Lord. I noticed that they often clapped their hands to express their joy and raised their arms in the air in adoration. It certainly was more emotional than anything I had ever been used to, even at Cliff College, but it was genuine and controlled.

Peter Scothern was a striking figure who spoke with conviction and authority. His sermon was long but powerful and interesting and I listened with rapt attention.

The crunch came when he invited sick people to go forward for ministry for healing. I held my breath in amazement. He moved among the people and as he laid his hands upon them, they fell to the ground as if under some immense power. The congregation were singing, 'Jesus is passing this way, passing this way. He's passing this way today.' In my imagination I could see Him actually doing that in His white robes, healing all that were sick with various diseases. The climax came when Peter Scothern urged a woman who had been confined to a wheel-chair for eleven years to 'rise and walk in the name of Jesus', which she did. Here was I, it seemed, seeing the Jesus of the Bible doing exactly the same things as He did two thousand years ago! I had seen people converted at Cliff College but never miraculously healed. This was a new dimension of Christianity as far as I was concerned.

After the meeting, I had a chance to speak to Peter Scothern and with tearful eyes I told him about the plight of my brother. 'Will you go and visit him?' I asked hopefully. 'You see, he's too sick to come to a meeting like this.' Peter said that he could make no promises, which disappointed me as his home in Mansfield was not too far from where George lay seriously ill in Nottingham. However, I realised that a man like Peter Scothern must be very busy and receive many such requests, and I was relieved when he promised that he would pray for him, in his absence.

The whole meeting had deeply impressed me and it was nearly midnight when I arrived home to a rather anxious husband, to whom I related the events of the evening with much excitement. To my surprise Trevor didn't pour cold water on my enthusiasm. 'This may be what I have been looking for all my Christian life,' he said, and he promised that the next time I went he would certainly go with me.

He was true to his word and we made several visits to that small Pentecostal Church, whether Peter Scothern was there or not. Sometimes Trevor even went by himself and it was after one such occasion that he arrived home and said that he had asked the elders to lay hands on him for the 'Baptism of the Holy Spirit', an infilling of spiritual power which he felt that he sadly lacked.

It was six weeks later, on 10th May 1969, that I returned home from a part-time job I was doing to find a husband excited and enraptured, his absolutely glowing face almost telling me its own story. 'I've had two hours in heaven,' he said. 'It seemed as if I had been lifted above the earth to heaven itself. I have been speaking in tongues and singing in the Holy Spirit. I felt at one stage that I ought to have left a message for you saying "Gone to heaven, back later".'

I was excited for him. Yet strangely enough I was the one who felt somewhat apprehensive and afraid. I knew my husband well enough to know that he didn't do anything by halves when it came to Christianity. I wondered what would happen next; where his new found experience would take us.

In the ensuing weeks I saw a transformation in my huband's life. He seemed to ooze love for me and his family. He preached with power and authority. He organised house-meetings for people in the Church who were seeking something deeper in their spiritual lives, though this brought him into conflict with the Vicar. One day he took me in his arms, looked at me so tenderly and said, 'Darling, I am sorry that we must be on the move. I must take this new experience into a parish of my own where I am sure I shall see God move in power.'

In the ensuing weeks my brother did in fact die, which brought me great grief. Peter Scothern had not visited him but another minister of divine healing had done so and laid hands on him. Miraculously, however, George died a Christan because of this experience. Tapes of miracle meetings had had a profound effect upon him. His passing did not make either myself or Trevor put aside all we had seen in the Pentecostal Church as phoney. We had discovered, we knew, something real and vital which enabled us to leave George in God's loving hands.

Trevor was, by now, in contact with the Bishop who eventually said that he could go and look at the parish of St. Paul's, Hainault, near London, with a view to going there to be Vicar. We went looking for the place one day and simply couldn't find the area, never mind the small almost pre-fabricated Church building which was down some back streets and behind the shopping parade. Hainault, we eventually found, was a large housing estate of some fourteen thousand people. I had only to look at the rows of council houses, mostly prefabricated, the streets, the schools and lastly the vicarage, to know that I would never want to live there. Trevor even wrote a letter to the Bishop saying that it was not the place for us. However, we went ahead with a meeting with the Church Council and Churchwarden.

It was when one of the Churchwardens said from 'out of the blue', 'Will you minister divine healing please if you come?' and another said, 'We would like to know more about the gifts of the Holy Spirit in Paul's first letter to the Corinthians,' that we knew God's Spirit had signified that He wanted us there. I still resisted, however, and heard Trevor saying, 'I feel I should go, but I can't go without a wife!'

That very night, at about four o'clock in the morning, I

suddenly shot up in bed and shouted, 'Trevor, I want to go to Hainault! I must go to Hainault!' God had given me a supernatural desire.

So it was that in August 1970, the van began to unload our furniture into the now renovated and redecorated vicarage. We had arrived and I was soon to find that I had been called to be a wife to a man who was to become a spiritual whirlwind. My own life too was going to change dramatically!

9: A Changed Wife

It was nearly three years later, as I sat in one of St. Paul's Church Tuesday Power, Praise and Healing Services that the Lord spoke to me in a way which I had not heard Him since the time at Cliff College when He told me that Trevor was to be my husband.

During these three years I had felt that I was growing more and more distant from Trevor. We had taken over a back-street parish consisting of a London 'overspill' housing estate. Very few people attended the Church and those who did were generally in middle life or older. The men had served in the Second World War and the estate had been hurriedly built to house them on their return from the fighting. We had found them to be, in the main, down-to-earth Londoners of working class, with hearts of gold. They just couldn't do enough for us, and Trevor sometimes had to restrain them lest they went beyond the Church's financial resources in order to help us. Their loving, caring attitude was beyond anything we had previously experienced. Even more important, they were eager to respond to the message of full life in the Holy Spirit which my husband brought to them.

The dynamic spiritual life which abounded in that Church, and which was eventually to be featured in every national newspaper, many periodicals, Christian journals and eventually on radio and television, didn't happen all at once. It was a slow process at first, but as miracles of healing and deliverance happened through Trevor's ministry, people began to flock to St. Paul's in their hundreds. They travelled from all over Britain and even different parts of the world. It was indeed a thrilling sight to behold up to six hundred worshippers packed into the small Church, all with arms uplifted, praising the Lord. Doctors began sending their patients to the Church and night after night scores of people were converted to Christ. The spiritual gifts of the New Testament era, such as tongues, interpretation, words of knowledge and wisdom, and singing in the Spirit, were much in evidence. Trevor was caught up in something bigger than himself or anything he had ever contemplated. His ministry now took every hour of his waking life. He was in demand to leave home to share the message with far-away churches and I, in more ways than one, was completely left behind.

I sat in the Church on that Tuesday evening and reflected on what had become my lot. True I had myself introduced my husband to the Pentecostal or Charismatic dimension of Christian life and ministry, but I had never thought it would become like this, certainly not in the Church of England! Over the years I had become a very traditional Anglican. I loved the sacraments of our Church, its Prayer Book and the whole way of life which it taught. In contrast, it seemed to me that what was happening at Hainault was neither respectable nor dignified! 'Whatever would the Bishop say,' I thought, 'If ever he should walk into all this emotionalism?'

On the outside I looked alright! Trevor had asked me to take charge of the counselling of the new converts or needy people and this was certainly done decently and in order, I saw to that! I could smile at people, half raise one arm to imitate the others, I had the status of being married to the Vicar. On the outside, everything seemed alright. Only I, and to some extent Trevor, knew what was going on inside me. After these seemingly glorious meetings, I would run out of the church in order to avoid having to talk to anyone. I would dash into the vicarage, curl up on the sofa and weep and weep and weep. Trevor would come in late and tired but there was no wife to welcome him with a cup of coffee. I had taken my unhappy self off to bed. It just couldn't go on.

I knew, deep down, the source of the trouble was

spiritual. I just couldn't relate my ordinary, proper, dignified Anglican life to the 'Charismatic experience'. Part of me longed for it because I could see the change for the better in the lives of those who were 'released' or 'baptised' in the Spirit. All my spiritual lines seemed to have become crossed and confused. I couldn't make sense of it at all, yet what was happening around me was obviously very real to everyone else. I just couldn't get any lower, I had to find God that night.

As I sat in the pew I determined to be *real* with God in a way I had never been since my conversion experience. You see, I was a proud and even stubborn person and I had to reach desperation point before I could really be helped by Him.

The healing ministry was finished and everyone had sat down. My husband was asking for the last time if there was anyone present who needed ministry. 'Now,' I thought, 'here is my God-given opportunity. *I am* going forward for the ministry of the laying-on-of-hands tonight.'

Almost immediately I heard a voice saying, 'Don't make a fool of yourself. You're alright. After all, you are the Vicar's wife, you love the Sacraments, you are married to Trevor Dearing. Don't do it.'

'Get thee behind me, Satan,' I replied, recognising that the temptation to remain seated was directly from the evil one.

Slowly I rose to my feet and went forward. I am still not sure who actually laid hands on me, whether it was Trevor or one of his friends.

'I want to be filled with the Holy Spirit,' I mumbled, half audibly, with my eyes firmly closed.

I felt hands being placed on my head. It all happened so quickly and without any emotion. It was a blissful experience as peace seemed to flood my entire being. Then it happened! Something I had said I would never do because I had something of a trained mind and was in charge of my emotions. I felt myself slowly falling to the ground! I don't know how long I lay there, but all I knew was that I soaked up the Holy Spirit as a sponge soaks up water. I rose groggily to my feet and returned to my seat.

'Thank you, Lord!' I whispered. 'In these moments I make myself totally available to you! Use me wherever and in whatever way you like.'

When I returned to the vicarage, I felt wonderfully light-hearted. No longer did I want to curl up and cry. I wanted to laugh and sing for joy. Trevor had a new wife and a cup of coffee waiting for him when he returned home. I was too excited to talk! However, when we went to bed I just couldn't stop singing songs of praise, and I started reading the Bible and just couldn't put it down. It seemed to be no longer in black and white but in colour and 3D. At about 4 a.m. Trevor became somewhat impatient and said, 'Can't you put the light off? I'm trying to go to sleep. I have an early appointment tomorrow.'

'I don't know what's happened to me,' I replied. 'I can't stop singing.'

'You've been baptised in the Holy Spirit,' he explained, 'but you don't have to just live for tonight. This experience will be with you for ever.'

Sure enough, the next morning, I still felt elated. On the phone or in the street, as opportunity arose, I found myself talking to people about Jesus. Before that time I had been able to talk to people about the Church or things related to the Church but had felt a sense of embarassment when I wanted to talk about Jesus. Now things were different. Hadn't He said, 'You will receive power. . . and you will be my witnesses'? This was the first of many releases I found in my new life in the Holy Spirit.

Prior to this experience, I had always been a very shy person, hardly daring even to lead the prayers at the Mothers' Union meetings. Now I found that, although I didn't initally speak in tongues, I was interpreting other people's tongues messages and beginning to step out in prophetic utterances I had also a sensitive gift of discernment, and knew whether or not people were under the rule of evil spirits.

Of course, I now experienced a new nearness to Trevor, for we were both experiencing the same 'in depth' experience of the Holy Spirit. We were one at the deepest level of spiritual life. Everything around me seemed to change as I saw it from a new perspective. I saw in a new way what it meant to be called to be a wife and a mother and that this was the highest call from God upon any woman's life. Housework, cooking, washing and ironing were transformed into avenues of service as I sang hymns and choruses around the house, even above the sound of my electric mixer or sweeper.

I was a released woman: released from spiritual hang-ups and bondages; released to praise God with uninhibited joy and to serve Him with new fervour. I found that nothing I cherished in Church of England worship and belief was taken from me. Quite the reverse, everything was filled with new meaning as I brought my new experience of the Spirit to the rituals and sacraments of the Church. 'My soul *doth* magnify the Lord and my spirit *hath* rejoiced in God my Saviour,' I was able to sing with upraised arms. The Lord whom I had seen at work in that Pentecostal Church and in St. Paul's was now at work in me! I was, I knew, being released and made ready for the wonderful new avenues of service He was preparing for me. I had been called to be a wife to a Spirit-filled husband, to give him up to God as a living sacrifice and to receive him back filled with love. I was now to share with him in his minstry in a deeper level than before, not only in Spirit-inspired counselling, but more amazingly, in the ministry of healing.

10: One Flesh in Ministry

By the September of 1975 it was obvious that the Lord was calling Trevor to a larger ministry even than that at St. Paul's. The steady streams of requests he had been receiving to take elsewhere his ministry of evangelism, teaching and healing, had now become a flood. He had been leaving the parish more and more in response to at least some of them, but the matter reached a head when he was invited to go to the diocese of Singapore for a six-week mission to the Anglican Churches there to introduce them to a deeper life in the Holy Spirit. This followed a visit to our Church by the then Bishop of Singapore, Chui Ban It, was to follow. In deciding to go, however, two significant changes took place which were vitally to affect both our lives, especially mine.

Firstly, our own Bishop, the Bishop of Chelmsford, asked Trevor to go to see him. Trevor went alone and came back with a new commission for his ministry. He and the Bishop had agreed together that Trevor was being called to leave the local setting of a parish in order to serve the wider Church in other parts of the world. Trevor, it was decided, would leave St. Paul's, Hainault, on his return from Singapore in order to take up this work. We would leave our home, the vicarage, and receive no salary but live by faith in God alone.

Secondly, the Bishop of Singapore was asking that I should accompany Trevor on the mission and that together with an organist who could play all the new Charismatic songs by ear, I would make up the team of three. It was in Singapore that my ministry alongside Trevor first began.

Our experience in Singapore was truly memorable for the

glory of God and the extension of His Kingdom. On this occasion I didn't engage in any speaking or healing ministry as I felt that was Trevor's ministry and in no way my own. However, I did share with Trevor in several other ways, especially in always being with him, sharing my story of God's work in my life in an informal way in the many homes to which we were invited.

The Singaporians were very loving and hospitable towards us. My main difficulty was the food. Trevor once said, 'If it walks, crawls, runs or swims and they can catch it, they will eat it!' I just couldn't even begin to eat things like frog's legs, shark's fins or snake skins. Eventually, I had to ask these dear people if they could find me English food or I would starve to death, especially as the Chinese food, so called, was nothing like that of the same name served up in Chinese restaurants in England! They obliged, but imagine my surprise when, on one occasion, I asked for chicken and that was exactly what I got—a whole chicken served up complete with neck, head and entrails. Our Chinese host asked if he could have the delicacy. When I agreed he split open the chicken's head with his chop-sticks and pulled out and ate its brain! At the same meal he told me that some elderly people, when young, would have eaten a whole mouse, dipped in wine, to renew their strength after having a baby! I ate nothing again at that meal! I didn't have a missionary stomach.

It was, however, a wonderful six weeks in the service of our Lord Jesus. I suppose the most demanding task I had to face was at the end when we were meeting in the Cathedral. Trevor was trying to introduce a flow of the gifts of the Holy Spirit at prayer meetings. We split the large crowd into two such meetings, one upstairs with Trevor as the leader and I was asked to lead the one downstairs, with the help of the Bishop! I suppose ours never really got off the ground. It was more like a silent Quaker meeting than a Charismatic prayer meeting. Upstairs, however, Trevor's group was having a real glory-time in the Holy Spirit. Eventually we left ours to join them in dancing in the Holy

Spirit. However I had been closely at Trevor's side for most events during those six weeks and I had begun to feel I might not only support him but actually minister with him.

On our return, we left St. Paul's, and worked with a group of friends from the Church in what was called the Power, Praise and Healing Mission. The Lord provided us with a loan with which we purchased a large house in Ilford, Essex, to be our home and the headquarters of the Mission. A charitable trust was established and we began to live 'by faith'. Soon we were finding that the Lord was providing for all our needs and eventually all our loans were paid off. From that day to this our testimony is that the Lord has kept us better than the Church of England ever did!

Despite all this I found this period of three years a real strain for me personally and in our relationship. The trouble was that our family of four children were still all at home and needed 'mother' in every way. Trevor, on the other hand, was spending several days at a time away from home on missions accompanied by his friends. They were good people and were doing their best to help Trevor in his much publicised and even televised ministry. However, I felt bereft and had a sinking feeling in my heart every time I waved him and the team goodbye and once again turned my attention, feeling somewhat lonely, to the care of the children.

Trevor's work with the Power, Praise and Healing Mission continued to grow in impetus. Gradually, I began to go with him, especially when those who wanted him to mission said that they liked us both together and found I was a real help in fellowship in their homes. Because of the children, however, these times were fewer than I would have desired. Sometimes I found someone to look after them on the longer missions. Various friends, including my mother, moved into the house so that I could be a wife to Trevor on his overseas tours. Continually, I found myself being pulled in two directions at once. When I was at home with the children, then I wanted to be with Trevor and felt that my place was at his side. However, when I was with him, I felt that as a mother I ought to be with the children. I felt torn in two. If it hadn't been for the help I found in my new experience of the Holy Spirit, I think I would have collapsed in a complete nervous breakdown. As it was, the grace of God saw me through this very difficult period.

Eventually, Jim Rattenbury, who was regarded as a real prophet in the team and who was Trevor's closest companion in these years, began to say that he felt that Trevor and I had a special ministry together. Eventually this came to pass in a new and deeper way when I was with Trevor and Jim at Wisbech in Cambridgeshire. Trevor was ministering the laying-on-of-hands to a large number of people and I was sitting in the congregation as usual, with my eyes closed, praying for his work. Suddenly I heard him say, 'Stop coming forward everyone! Please stop the music and singing because something new is going to happen this evening.' I sat up, wondering what this new thing could be.

'The Lord has just shown me,' continued Trevor, 'that my wife has a share in my healing ministry and I am now asking her to come forward and begin to lay hands upon the sick.'

I felt momentarily that I would die with shock! However, there was nothing to do but comply with his request. I couldn't argue in front of all these people! Trevor told me later that, if my look could have killed, then he would have needed immediate healing ministry! Slowly I rose to my feet and joined him at the front of the Church.

'Lay hands on that man over there, please,' he said to me, 'and just pray for him as you feel led.'

The man was over six feet tall and weighed, I guessed, over fourteen stones. He was huge. I stood on the tips of my toes in order to reach his head and had no sooner touched him than, to my astonishment, he collapsed to the ground under the power of the Holy Spirit. He rose to declare publicly that he had been instantaneously healed of severe pain in his back! My healing ministry alongside my husband had begun. A new phase in our 'one-flesh' relationship in the Lord had been inaugurated by the Holy Spirit.

It was soon after this that Trevor and I set out on another ministry tour in the USA. However, this time it was different. From the beginning to the end it was a thoroughly joint ministry in healing and counselling. I began also to speak in public, sharing my testimony to the way in which the Holy Spirit had filled and changed my life. I constantly remembered the promise I had made to the Lord, that I would be wholly available for Him. Now He was using me with Trevor in a dynamic way.

11: A Woman's Ministry

I have always felt, both from an 'inward witness' as well as from the teaching of the Bible, that men should hold the place of leadership in the home and in the Church. I have always felt that they should, with occasional exceptions, be the ministers of the Word and especially of the Sacraments of the Church. However, that has never meant for me that women should have no ministry at all, but that they should willingly make themselves available for whatever the Lord would have them do for the service of his Kingdom. The Bible itself preaches that God will bestow spiritual gifts upon women who are surrendered to Him and willing to receive them, as for instance Philip's daughters who prophesied (Acts 21:9).

I have never been a person who has felt the urge to push myself forward to minister for the Lord. By nature I would rather sit on a back seat in the Church and enjoy the ministry of others. The Lord has had to make it very clear to me when He has wanted me to serve Him 'at the front'. When He has, then I have been willing to obey Him in whatever He has given me to do.

I could accept that He wanted me to serve alongside Trevor as his wife, because after all, we had been fused into 'one flesh' by Him. I have always wanted to feel myself 'covered' by Trevor during such ministry and have never in any way wanted to dominate in our ministry together. I have always taken the 'lower place' beside or behind my husband and many people have expressed to us how beautiful it is to see a relationship like this in a man and wife team ministry. They have often commented that they have felt 'put off' by strong women exerting themselves over and beyond their husbands when ministering together for the Lord.

When Trevor and I returned from our visit to America, where for the first time we had flowed together in ministry, we felt we had to share with the Power, Praise and Healing Mission that Trevor and I felt that the Lord had now called us to minister together in a special way and that, in future, we should minister as Trevor and Anne Dearing Renewal Ministeries. We hoped that we would still have close fellowship links with the Mission, especially with those who lived in our area, but this wasn't to be. Eventually, we moved from our home in Ilford to my home town of Stamford in Lincolnshire, where we had always wanted one day to live, and so our new joint ministry came into being.

By this time the Lord had so blessed us that we were able quickly to pay off all the money we owed to our friends for our house. We owned a very servicable car and had enough money to be unhindered by any financial concerns, and we were overwhelmed with requests to minister in England and all over the world. Our children had now grown up and had 'left the nest', only our son Philip still needing parental care. So I was much more free to minister with Trevor on our missions. The Lord contrived to use me in the giving of my testimony at meetings, in laying hands upon the sick and occasionally in the gift of interpretation of tongues. In this sort of relationship Trevor and I began to enjoy some wonderful times of ministry together.

One such occasion was when Trevor was asked to be the final speaker at a World Conference of the Holy Spirit in Jerusalem. It was a remarkable time of ministry because, following Trevor's message on 'The Foolishness of God', the Holy Spirit began to move in power. We never did really start laying hands on people because the Lord began to heal people Himself, without any human help! However, just as Trevor was closing the meeting, I felt the urge to prophesy. I had never been used in this way before but once again I made myself available to the Lord and I remember saying words along these lines.

'I have moved in power amongst you, says the Lord. You have seen my glory; glory as of One Risen from the dead, crowned with honour, at the Father's right hand. Yet there are those amongst you who have not responded to Me. I call upon my children, my beloved people of old, the Jews, to hear My voice and own Me as Messiah. I brought you here for this very purpose, because I have chosen you, in order that you may know Me and call upon My Name. Come to Me *now*.'

As soon as I stopped speaking about forty people, not only Jews but Arabs too, left their seats and, with faces flooded with tears, knelt at the front of the auditorium to yield their lives to Jesus as Lord. It was a deeply moving occasion and as I looked at them, I could barely realise that God Himself had used my mouth through which to speak. The Lord continued to use me in this way, specifically giving me the word of knowledge about persons who still need to answer His call. So I have been used beyond my wildest dreams to bring people to Christ. I am not a preacher, nor an evangelist, but God has given me spiritual gifts at His chosen times to use me as a soulwinner.

Another remarkable incident took place when I was ministering with Trevor at a World Conference of the Holy Spirit in Switzerland. Many hundreds of people had gathered to hear Trevor preach and then move into healing. I took my place by his side and began to minister to people by myself. Many nations and languages were represented and so we couldn't always make use of an interpreter.

The next day two ladies approached me after breakfast. One spoke both Spanish and English fluently, the other spoke no English at all. I was asked if I spoke Spanish and, of course, replied in the negative. 'That's remarkable,' exclaimed the English speaking lady, 'truly a miracle has happened.'

'You see,' she explained, 'my Spanish friend here came to you for ministry and without asking her any questions, you began to pray for her bad back. You also told her that she was suffering from depression because of a curse upon her life due to the fact that her mother had been a spiritist medium. You set her free from that curse and today she is a different person. She only came to the Conference as an observer, but has now accepted Jesus Christ as her personal Saviour. She has been convinced of God's power because, although in my hearing you spoke to her in English, she understood every word you said, because she heard you in Spanish!' It had been just like the miracle of tongues at Pentecost all over again. The Spanish lady had also been wonderfully healed by the power of God.

Perhaps the most momentous miracle in my own ministry occurred when Trevor and I were missioning in Finland. How those Finnish people packed into the Churches. I can even remember one night when hundreds stood outside the church because it was packed to capacity. They waited patiently outside until Trevor had finished his message but all began to crowd around us as soon as they knew that the healing ministry had begun. Trevor and I were pressed back almost to the walls of the church and were laying hands on people who were falling to the ground under the power of the Holy Spirit the moment we touched them. It was difficult to grasp what was happening at the time, especially when one lady rose from the floor and began shouting excitedly in Finnish and running around the Church. It was months later that we received a copy of a Finnish Christian periodical in which it was recounted that this woman, previously totally blind, with the retinas of her eyes destroyed, had received her sight! Glory be to Jesus!

It has often been the case that I have only heard what the Lord has graciously done through my ministry many months after the event. At subsequent meetings in the same area folk have told me just how their lives were changed as I layed my hands upon them. The incidents are too many to record but they include everything from the physical healing of cancers, the restoration of marriage relationships, the miraculous healing of the infirm and crippled, and the immediate release of people from such long-standing emotional distresses as agoraphobia and chronic depression.

Only this month as I write, American friends have sent me a copy of the widely circulated *Guideposts* magazine in which is related the wonderful change that occurred in a man's life in Saybrook, when Trevor and I were missioning in America more than three years ago. It seems that Paul had many problems which had resulted in marital separation. However, his wife Deb had found Christ and the union had been restored. She longer for her husband to find the Saviour, for she knew that in Him lay the only hope of a permanent solution. She wrote:

'Then a visiting clergyman from England, the Reverend Trevor Dearing, came to our Church. I thought Paul might be interested in hearing a speaker from another part of the world. But when I told Paul about Father Dearing I could see the old fire rise in his eyes and I quickly backed off.

However, on the following Sunday, as I was leaving for Church, Paul stopped me at the door. "I'll go with you," he said, adding quickly, "But just this once."

I was elated, but hid my feelings. Once in Church I could sense his resistance to everything that was taking place. He sat there stiff, scowling, silent when the hymns were sung. He heard the call to the altar, watched people answer it. Then, to my amazement, Paul rose slowly and moved down the aisle. "Oh, Lord, he needs Your help," I prayed. But when the clergyman placed his hands on Paul's head, he just stiffly stood there, turned and hurried back to my side.

On the way home he was silent for a time, then quietly said, "I walked down the aisle because I wanted to cleanse myself of all the wrong I did and the hurt I gave you. But when Father Dearing put his hands on my head I was skeptical that anything could happen. Deb, I just couldn't open my heart."

I prayed for the right words to say. "Will. . . will you come with me again?" I ventured.

"Maybe. I don't know." And then he added almost

under his breath, "I've watched you over the past year, Deb, and you've become so sure, so serene. I wish I could feel the way you do."

'The following Sunday night Paul decided on his own to attend the prayer meeting in Church. Father Dearing and his wife, Anne, were at the altar. When Father Dearing began talking, Paul listened intently. He hunched forward when Father Dearing talked of our inner prison, a prison of our own making. We all want to escape it, but even the most powerful cannot escape alone. There is only One who can give us the key. Then he invited everyone who had not yet met Jesus to come and meet Him.

Paul stood up. His face was pale, his eyes shining, his fingers gripped my arm. "Deb, come with me," he said softly. I rose and he placed me in front of him, still holding my arm. We followed the first few people down the aisle. At the altar he stood behind me. I heard a noise. I turned. Paul lay on the floor. People were praying over him. Then he got up slowly and led me back to our seats. He was alright but I was mystified as to what had happened to him.

When the meeting was over Paul hurried both of us outside.

"I wasn't sure anything would happen," he said, his face flushed, his speech rapid, as though he wanted to tell it all at once.

"But when Mrs Dearing put her hands on my head, I felt a surge of peace sweep through me like a big ocean wave. All my strength left me. Next thing I knew I was on my back, looking up at a ring of faces praying. My mind cleared and I knew I had surrendered myself to the presence of God."

Paul's face was filled with a new light. He looked serene, at peace. He crushed me to him and said huskily, "Deb, I felt as if I was resting in the hands of the Lord!"

"You *were*, Paul," I said joyously. "You are!"

Since that day, God's hand has been on Paul. His inner turmoil is gone. Of course, our problems didn't all

disappear, nor did our marriage become all sweetness and light. But now the two of us are working on them together.
(*Guideposts*, August 1985)

So, the Lord had been graciously pleased to use my ministry, I would guess, on many occasions.

However, I have not always ministered alongside Trevor, although I still feel this to be my rightful place in ministry. At times God has used me by myself, especially in ministry to women. On such occasions, even when Trevor hasn't been there, I have still felt his spiritual covering over me.

At women's meetings, often in homes, remarkable events have taken place as I, basically a nervous person, have shared with them my experience of the Lord and the power of the Holy Spirit. As I have said, I have never been a preacher, so I have simply given my testimony as to how the Lord had to deal with a 'respectable' Vicar's wife, who was both stubborn and proud, in order to heal me fully and deeply and then use me. I have then offered ministry to the women present. Somehow the Lord has used my words to penetrate their frequently self-sufficient exteriors and reach the need of their inner lives. Many have broken down and wept openly as the Lord has touched them.

I can well remember such a meeting in Bermuda, when the Lord also used me to heal a very sick cat of which I still have a photograph, fit and well! At another I remember I was feeling rather apprehensive as I was facing a group of rather austere-looking Anglican ladies who, on the surface, didn't seem at all ready to receive a message about baptism in the Holy Sprit. Once again, however, I simply shared my own testimony and offered ministry. They soon began to respond, fall under the power of the Spirit and weep openly as God moved amongst them. I was very late home for lunch that day as I was ministering to women for over two hours.

The Lord has also used Trevor and me in counselling together. In fact Trevor doesn't like counselling any woman without my being there. Often the Lord has given me the word of knowledge or wisdom to set the person free. Frequently I have counselled women alone, feeling this to be a ministry the Lord has given to me. I have especially, by God's grace, been able to help Vicars' and Christian Ministers' wives, as I identify with them so easily in their feelings of isolation and in their needs as they face responsibilites for which they are so often unprepared when they become married.

I have been given a particular gift of discernment in relation to the presence—or often absence—of evil spirits in the lives of those seeking ministry. One memorable occasion was when I was called to a house where a youth meeting was taking place. An urgent call had come to our home asking for help. It seemed that the leaders had been trying to cast an evil spirit out of a boy without success for nearly two hours. I went ahead of Trevor who was otherwise engaged. I walked into the room and immediately sensed that this was not a case for deliverance.

'Get up,' I ordered the young man laying on the floor. 'Stop pretending and face the *real* problems in your life.'

I then suggested that the hostess should give him and everyone else a cup of tea. Quickly the young man got up, behaving normally, and calm was restored. I must say, however, that despite my gift of discernment I have always felt that it is Trevor's ministry actually to cast out evil spirits. I feel it is a man's job. So often I have discerned and then he has cast out evil from peoples' lives, and the glory has been all the Lord's.

Perhaps the most memorable of all occasions on which I ministered by myself was in Singapore. We had been asked to visit Singapore for a second time and Trevor had gone ahead of me for two weeks' ministry by himself, as I felt I had to stay for a while with our son Philip. Eventually, I took the seventeen-and-a-half-hour flight alone and on the flight developed a terrible migraine. I arrived in Singapore nauseated, in pain and feeling very ill. I was met by the Bishop and taken to the hotel where Trevor was staying and to which he had just returned following a meeting. I explained to him just how ill I felt and I could see anxiety creep all over his face.

'I am so sorry you are feeling so ill, darling,' he said in the presence of the Bishop, 'and you being ill has caused us another problem. I arrived to find that tomorrow evening I have been booked for two meetings, one at a Church and the other in a hotel at a Full Gospel Businessmen's gathering. We were hoping that we could split up for the evening and you could take the meeting at the hotel.'

He and the Bishop laid hands on me and I then laid my throbbing head on the pillows of the bed. Today was bad enough, I would have to trust the Lord for the morrow.

The next day my migraine had subsided but I felt very weak as I set off by car for the Hilton Hotel without Trevor, to speak to the Singapore Full Gospel Businessmen's Fellowship. To my amazement the hotel ballroom was packed. Trevor, I knew, would be well into his meeting, and he had promised to finish as early as possible and hurry to help me with the ministry. It was reassuring yet at the same time a little disconcerting to have our friend Chui Ban It, the Bishop of Singapore, sitting beside me. He too had promised to help in the ministry.

I stood up to speak, feeling rather weak at the knees, but then felt the presence of the Lord really with me. I shared my testimony, telling them how God had dealt with me on that evening years before in St. Paul's Church, London. I described the blessing that there had been on my life ever since. I offered ministry to all who wished to receive the power of the same Spirit into their lives. The ministry in fact didn't take long because everyone was falling down under the power of the Holy Spirit the moment I touched them. When Trevor arrived it was not to help in the ministry but to discover that the meeting was over and to pick his way amidst all the bodies that were lying on the floor. He didn't find me ill and exhausted but wonderfully blessed and refreshed. We later learned that God had moved in many ways in the lives of people that evening to save, heal and anoint.

The ministry the Lord had given me by myself has proved to be primarily amongst women, but He has shown through such events as those in Singapore that He will endow and use me on other occasions when Trevor cannot be with me. However, from the beginning and still today I feel that my ministry is mainly alongside my husband and that He has called us into a special ministry 'in harness' together, as one-flesh in Him. I am sure He foresaw this wonderful joint-mission for Him even before I sat at the water-pump in Barnack and said, 'I want to marry a parson.' In these last years He alone knows all that He has accomplished through our joint ministry. Observers have often commented that, in the way I minister with Trevor—not pushing as a 'strong' woman, but waiting upon his suggestions, and doing that which together we feel truly to be in the Spirit—I have complemented my husband's ministry. Those who have known us since the earliest days of Trevor's baptism in the Holy Spirit say that he never seemed complete in ministry without me on those occasions when he has had, for family reasons, to be alone. Since we began ministry together, I have never felt left behind, alone or isolated, but I have felt one-flesh with my husband in the deepest possible way. Truly, it is wonderful to be called to be a wife!

12: 'In Sickness'

It was whilst we were engaging in our joint ministry in Florida. USA, that the possibility was first raised of our moving to Seattle to succeed the Rev. Dennis Bennett as rector of St Luke's Episcopal Church, Seattle. Trevor had begun to feel tired through fulfilling our full schedule of itinerant ministry and felt he needed to have a rest and a 'touch-base' with a pastoral ministry again. He was beginning to show signs of stress both emotionally and physically and our doctor in England felt sure that a change of ministry was needed and that then all would be well. The prospect of being rector at the famous Church of St Luke's, which we knew to be thoroughly Charismatic, seemed possibly to be the lord's answer to the need.

We would, I am sure, not have thought of leaving England had the opportunity arisen of becoming a vicar here. In fact, it was quite the reverse. Trevor's contact with Bishops at home about the possibility of having a parish had proved fruitless. Two said that they couldn't conceive of there ever being a parish that would be 'suitable' for Trevor's Charismatic ministry. The Bishop of Chelmsford, who had first helped to send us out on our faith ministry, had written that it would not be possible for Trevor to return to the Chelmsford Diocese because a 'certain mythology' surrounded his name in the area! Doors in England seemed to be closed and a door in America opening.

When a rector first raised the matter with us in Florida, Trevor told him to inform the Church in Seattle that he was very open to the idea. We hadn't been back in England long before the Churchwardens of St. Luke's Episcopal Church were in touch with us to discuss the idea. We had a three-way hour's transatlantic telephone interview with them one Sunday evening and it was decided that we should fly out to Seattle for a week to view the parish and discuss the matter further.

We went out to Seattle in March 1981, and had a wonderful time of fellowship with the Church there and felt the warmth of their love and acceptance. Still, however, both they and we had to seek the Lord's will further as there was at least one person on their Search Committee with reservations and we ourselves had to finally make up our minds. Certainly it looked a most attractive and exciting proposition.

On our return home, the implications of our proposed move began to dawn upon us, especially in relation to our children. Rebecca was married, Rachael was engaged to be married, Ruth was nursing and said she would never want to come to the USA. Our son Philip also faced a dramatic change in his education as he was about to take his 'O' levels at the fine Grammar School in Stamford. Trevor and I would be tearing up roots that had been thrust deep into British soil for more than forty years. We began to be disquieted.

Two factors finalised our decision to make the move. Firstly, at the American end the new Vestry at St. Luke's were now unanimous about our going and the Bishop of Olympia, who had previously interviewed us, gave the venture his warmest blessing. At our end, we put our house on the market and it immediately sold at the price which we were asking. The Church agreed to pay for all our furniture to be taken out to the USA. Accomodation was easily arranged for Philip for the nine months he would need it, and the Church stated they would finance a twice-yearly return to England to see our family. In short, there was not one impediment in the way of our going to take up the appointment in Seattle. We were even given special visa clearance by the American Embassy in London. Surely all the signs were saying 'Thus saith the Lord—Go!'

Trevor and I arrived at Seattle airport in the June of 1981

to receive a wonderfully warm welcome from the Church. They met us with banners such as 'Mash the tea, the British are here' and 'Welcome Dearings to St. Luke's'. Balloons filled the air around us. We were driven to our new home, the rectory, to use borrowed furniture and equipment until ours arrived six weeks later.

Despite this good start things soon began to go wrong. The pound sterling had fallen badly against the dollar and we hadn't enough money to buy the house we had intended, or to buy the rectory. Philip and Rachael came over and for different reasons decided to make their home in the USA. We couldn't refuse them. A year later Ruth, a nurse, made the same decision. This would not have mattered, especially as the Church Vestry and the wonderful St. Luke's people were doing everything possible to make us feel at home and the Church was responding wonderfully to Trevor's ministry and re-organisation of its life. The problem was Trevor's health.

Within three weeks of our arrival he had experienced his first uncontrollable attack of panic, which shook his whole being. It reminded him of the severe illness he had suffered for eight years in his adolescence. Steadily his health began to deteriorate. He was experiencing a lot of physical pain, especially in his chest. He was under constant medical care, sometimes rushed as an emergency into hospital, suffered haemorrhages, and eventually daily dreadful panic attacks. He was taking medication and battling courageously on with his work for the Lord which was bearing more and more fruit. Eventually, he underwent an operation to examine his heart, was diagnosed as having coronary artery disease and coronary artery spasms—but still he worked on.

It is difficult to describe what it was like to be a wife during this period in America. I have never felt more isolated, concerned, anxious and distressed in the whole of my life. I had a sick husband and responsibility for a family, and was exercising a ministry in the Church, in a strange country thousands of miles away from Stamford, the place where I felt truly at home. Many dear people in the Church of St. Luke's helped as best they could, but in the end it was that simple faith in God that I have always had since a child which sustained, comforted and strengthened me. His grace was made perfect in weakness as I was constantly by my husband's side ministering to him who was now hardly able to help himself.

I couldn't count how many hours I have spent since December 1981 in ministering, encouraging and reassuring him. I couldn't count how many hours I spent in hospitals by his bedside, or forget how many times he was rushed into hospital for what could have been his last hours on earth. Telephoning for emergency ambulance services and waiting in Emergency Rooms in hospitals became almost part of my life. I loved him, cared for him and watched him grow increasingly ill. It could hardly have been more difficult, facing culture shock, spiritual culture shock, being far away from family and seeing my husband deteriorate. Deep down, however, I had a promise from the Lord, a witness to my spirit from heaven above: 'Do not fear, my child, for I will not let him die.' At times the Voice seemed to be overwhelmed by anxiety, but it was never drowned out of my spirit.

Matters came to a head in March 1983. Trevor had felt that he might be better if he fulfilled his calling as an evangelist whilst being pastor at St. Luke's. Accordingly, he arranged some missions, the first of which was to be held at the Church of the Resurrection, Dallas, Texas. We had been there twice before and felt it would be a good place to begin. It meant my leaving the work of divine healing at St Luke's, over which Trevor had placed me in charge, in the hands of someone else but that, I thought, would be a small price to pay for Trevor's return to health.

In fact, quite the reverse happened. I watched my husband rapidly losing the battle with his panic attacks as the weekend went on. He became increasingly weak. At the end of the mission he was in a state of collapse and I wondered if we would make the flight home. We felt it would be unwise to share Trevor's illness with the loving

Dallas people or he would have been hospitalized hundreds of miles away from home. I held his hand, talked with him and sought to encourage him on what seemed an endless flight back to Seattle. At last he stumbled into the rectory and collapsed in sheer exhaustion upon the bed.

The next day we saw a specialist who immediately admitted Trevor into the Cabrini Towers Hospital in Seattle. After extensive tests it was shown that Trevor's body-chemistry had become completely imbalanced, caused by several years of much over-work and travel in his service for the Lord. He had coronary artery disease and was suffering artery spasms. Apparently, he had inherited a tendency to this illness from his father, but it had been sparked off by his over-work. The illness, we were told, was treatable but incurable.

Eventually, Trevor was released from hospital, under medication, but was absolutely incapable through weakness of doing any work. As usual he tried, but this time failed to make a come-back. We were reminded in the Scriptures of the way Paul had to leave Trophimus weak (Greek 'asthenes') at Miletus. Trevor was in the same condition! I nursed, and nursed, and nursed him in his sickness.

The people and Vestry at St. Luke's loved us and cared for us. They so wanted us to be able to continue the fruitful work we had done there. One of the Churchwardens stated that Trevor had done twenty years' work in two! At last they granted Trevor at least three months' leave of absence to see if he could get well. We decided to take this in England and so landed, once again, at Heathrow Airport. Some dear friends of ours, Dennis and Iris Rose, had managed to obtain an old gate-house in a rural part of Lincolnshire where Trevor could relax completely. However, even there he had to be under medical supervision and was again sent into hospital as an emergency. I spent hours beside him once again, but this time in a British hospital.

By the middle of May it had become obvious to us that there was no way Trevor would be able to give a date for returning to work. He was put on a disability pension by both the American and British Episcopal Churches and it seemed he would never work again. I had never in my wildest imagination dreamt what it would mean when, twenty-six years earlier, I had stood by his side in Barn Hill Methodist Church and said, 'I take this man to be my wedded husband. . . in sickness and in health.'

Trevor had become convinced that his primary calling was that of an evangelist rather than a pastor and that, having done what the Lord had wanted him to accomplish at St. Luke's, he was being called back to England. However, in June 1983 he was not fit to do anything and I had some more very demanding tasks to undertake as his wife.

13: 'To Have and to Hold'

On the day Trevor wrote out his resignation as rector of St. Luke's Church, I was with him in our sanctuary in the lodge in Lincolnshire. However, three of our four children, and all our clothes and furniture were in Seattle. It was a terrible time for all of us. I used a public telephone in Stamford Post Office to phone the children in Seattle to tell them the decision we had had to make. I spoke to Ruth who was twenty-five years of age and had been left 'in charge' of Rachael (twenty) and Philip (sixteen), with church members having promised to keep an eye on them. I spoke to all the children in turn and could sense the insecurity and dismay and distress which had now entered their lives.

It had almost been a tearing of my flesh in any case to leave them for three months in order to be with Trevor in England, to help him to get well. Now I felt like crying for them. how desperately we prayed that the Lord would sustain us all.

My next task was to return by myself and arrange for the removal of the furniture back to England. In the meantime we had to find and buy a house here for the furniture and us to live in! Trevor was just well enough to drive a car and begin our search for a new home. We did see the Bishop of Chelmsford to see if he could suggest any plans for our future but he couldn't and so Trevor was to stay 'disabled' and a pensioner at the age of fifty!

The Lord guided us to a new house which was being completed in a village one-and-a-half miles from Stamford, and we set about purchasing it and making it ready to be our new home. It was set in a very quiet place with a lovely country aspect, and was just right to help in Trevor's recovery to health. Once the purchase had been arranged I flew back to Seattle, to see our anxious children and arrange the furniture transportation. I must admit, however, that I was so exhausted upon my arrival in Seattle, having left my sick husband in the care of my mother, that I could do nothing at all except rest for nearly a week. After this time I was refreshed enough to engage in all my tasks for our removal back to England.

It was to prove to be only a partial removal because Rachael now announced her engagement to an American, Jim Payne, with whom she had been friendly for some time. They informed me that they planned to be married in America in the September and live in the States. Ruth, our nursing daughter, said that England only held a bleak future for her and that she would be staying in America to 'see how things worked out'. Our son Philip had reluctantly to return with us as he was under age.

The next ten days in Seattle were hectic. St Luke's were very loving and generous and said that they would pay for the furniture to be returned to England. I had a big job to do in listing all our goods for insurance purposes, and arranging the practicalities of the removal. I also had to see Ruth and Rachael securely established in a new apartment, giving them some of our furniture in order to make it 'home'. I had to see that tentative arrangements for the wedding were in hand, and attend Philip's Graduation Ceremony from Ballard High School. A crisis occurred when we realised that all his special clothes for the occasion had been accidentally shipped to England. The Lord answered prayer when my neighbour was able to fit him out from her son's wardrobe! I was asked to attend Church and say 'farewells' on behalf of Trevor and myself and thus leave the most loving, kind and generous people we had ever met. The most difficult, heart-rending task was to say goodbye to my beloved daughters who were huddled in a corner of the terminal building in tears. It was with a heavy heart, therefore, that I stepped onto the plane to return to Trevor, whom I had promised 'to have and to hold'.

He was at the airport to greet me and tell me of the moves to get our house straight. I ploughed into this task and, thankfully, it was ready to receive the furniture on the day it arrived back from the USA. Philip became a trainee accountant at a local firm and we were thankful to God that he had found work when so many yound people in the area were unemployed.

I worked hard, Trevor helping when he could, to make our new house a home. It seemed I had hardly had 'time to breathe' when September arrived and once again, alone, I set out for America to be at Rachael's wedding to represent her father and the whole family. The wedding itself was all planned by Rachael and Jim, with wonderful help from his parents and the folks at St. Luke's. I had never felt more alone.

This feeling of isolation was in no way occasioned by my American friends, who were delighted to see me and entertained me in a wonderful way. However, I was desperately missing Trevor. This was even more so on the actual day of the wedding as I walked into Church and was escorted to my seat to sit all alone on the front row. Tears flooded my eyes as I saw Rachael being escorted down the Church by Jim's father and not my husband. I felt I just couldn't see the wedding through. It was at my lowest moment that I felt as though an arm went round me and fingers squeezed into the upper part of my right arm. I heard a voice saying, 'I am Jesus. I am with you to strengthen you and I will be your friend and a husband to you. I will hold you up. Take courage and be at peace.' Almost immediately I felt a deep sense of comfort. My tears stopped flowing. The Lord whom I had known since I was a little girl at Barnack was still the same forty years later and I could feel His strength pouring into my being. From that moment I was happy. The reality of this experience will be with me until the end of my days. My Lord is my strength.

I flew back home and Trevor, Philip and I continued to settle into our new home. I was thrilled to be back with Trevor, all my tasks completed. I also began to see a wonderful healing taking place within him as together we waited upon the Lord to renew his strength. Eventually Papworth Hospital said that he didn't have any coronary artery disease and the spasms stopped. It was a gradual process through which the Lord was restoring him and teaching us many lessons. The other medical specialists were beginning to be very pleased with Trevor's progress. True, he became exhausted very easily and he had to be very careful not to undertake any demanding work, but he was definitely improving.

In March 1984 our medical advisers suggested it would be good for Trevor to speak and eventually to minister at some engagements. They felt it would be therapeutic for him. So Trevor and Anne Dearing Renewal Ministeries was reformed. The same year saw the publication of his book *God and the Healing of the Mind*, and in 1985 he was able to publish his sixth entitled *A People of Power* and then to help me with this one.

We began at occasional ministeries throughout England to minister together in a closer way than ever before. Our experience of sharing the valley of Trevor's sickness, with my 'having and holding' him, had, we found, enriched the spiritual harmony between us and we have flowed together in the Spirit in a deeper way than ever before. It seems now that the Lord uses Trevor to teach and preach and gives him words of knowledge about needs and special people God wishes to bless. I also sometimes have words that flow with his, but, unlike Trevor, am used more than ever before to bring healing to the sick through the laying-on-of-hands. We are truly one-flesh in every aspect of our marriage and ministry.

We do miss our two daughters who live in the USA a great deal, especially now Ruth has also married an American, another wedding I attended without Trevor. We praise God, however, for our three Christian sons-in-law. We have the consolation also of seeing our daughter in London, with her husband and our two grandchildren. Philip also is doing well and maturing into a fine young man. Trevor's health slowly continues to improve as he 'paces' his work, but it is thrilling to be back in ministry together again, still in constant contact with all our children and friends at St. Luke's. How grateful we are for God's goodness to us, and for such a lovely place to live and thrilling ministry to fulfil having and holding one another, knowing that this will be so until 'death us do part'.

14: 'Those whom God hath Joined Together'

It is possible to interpret these words from the marriage service in two ways. One is to say that at the most solemn moment in the ceremony, God is actually joining the two people so that they are one flesh. This is certainly true. However, it is possible to see behind the words an expression of God's sovereign rule over those two individuals so that it was by His choice and decree that they actually met and came to know each other and so were destined to be married. As I look back over my life I see God's sovereignty in many ways.

To begin with, I ask myself, when did I actually become a Christian? In the fullest sense of the word, I suppose it was when I was 'baptised in the Spirit' at St. Paul's, Hainault. Evangelicals will say it was at the time when I raised my hand in acceptance of Him in Ketton Methodist Church. But what about the time when, as a little girl, I sat and gazed at the crucifix in Barnack Parish Church, or when I said 'I want to marry a parson', or when I was confirmed or baptised as a baby? As I look back I can see that God's choice lay upon my life from as long as I can remember. I cannot think of a time when I did not have a belief that He existed and cared for me. I have asked many Christians about their experience of salvation, and on reflection they have all acknowledged the truth of Jesus' words, 'You did not choose me, but I chose you' (John 15:16). As Paul would say 'We were chosen in Him before the foundation of the world' (Eph. 1:4).

Experience has taught me that it is all too easy, in the light of some new, dramatic encounter with God, to dismiss our past knowledge of him as unimportant, or even worthless. So many people do this when giving their testimonies. I am sure that this is a mistake. It is easy to deny the path which God used, and continues to use, to bring us to ever deeper life with Him. I am sure I was chosen to belong to God, not of my deserving, ever since I was born.

I see, therefore, God's sovereign will at work in bringing together the paths of Trevor's life and my own. He knew us both and destined us for each other. I knew that I would recognise God's man for me as soon as I had met him and this proved to be true. Sadly, teenage girls and young women are often so afraid of being 'left on the shelf' that they rush into marriage. Young men too can be so physically attracted to one of the opposite sex that they too rush into marriage. In these and other cases, God's will is not truly sought and so the couple 'marry in haste and repent at leisure'. The terrible divorce rate these days, and the dreadful stress in marriages, even among Christians, show the extent to which believers have succumbed to the world and not sought God's will.

There can be no greater factor for stability in marriage than to know that God joined us together and planned the marriage from the day we were born. Maybe the way I looked out for my partner and waited until I was in my 'twenties before finding him may seem unusual, but I believe it should be every Christian's experience. God's sovereignty is surely at work in this vital aspect of the lives of believers, or He is not active at all! It has been my conviction that I married 'in the Lord' that has upheld me through the trials of life, Trevor's ministry, his absences, and even his sickness. God gave me this man and gave me to him!

Then, of course, looking back I can see the way He kept me through my terrible childhood sickness of chronic bronchitis, through the temptations of the world which were all around me whilst training as a nurse, the escapes I had from danger whilst hitch-hiking, and I am sure He guarded me from many 'hidden dangers, toils and deaths' of which I shall be unaware until I get to heaven. It is because I can see His sovereign Hand over me in the past that I can be confident that He has gone ahead to prepare my future.

There are, it seems, a few women who have to accept that it is God's will for them to be single for various reasons. This too can be seen, not as an accident, but according to His purpose. It would take several books to write of the wonderful service rendered to the Kingdom by those I have known personally, who have accepted single life as God's call. It is these especially, though not exclusively, who are called to full-time service in the Church.

Of course, God's perfect will does not always come to pass here on earth. Sometimes events take place which are surely the work of the devil or the result of our wrong choosing and mistakes. Still, however, the sovereignty of God overrules because He can work *all* things together for *good* for those who love Him and are called according to His purposes (Romans 8:28). If we face life positively with Him we can know that every moment can be a sacrament which, if we accept it rightly, can be used by God to work his purposes in and through our lives. This applies when people who have become Christians have been through the horrors of divorce, or to Christians married to a non-Christian partner. The Bible teaches that the unbelieving husband is sanctified through the believing wife's faith and that because of it, even her children are holy.

A submission to God's sovereignty and to all He has said in the Bible, His word, is at the very heart of victorious Christian living. How can a man, who has not really submitted to God's Lordship, really love his wife to the same extent as Christ loved the Church, 'loving it and giving Himself up for it' (Eph. 5)? A woman needs such love, her very nature calls out for it. How can a woman who has not submitted to Christ, submit to her husband (Eph. 5)? A woman needs love, a man needs respect, to affirm their natures. This is what God knows to be the case, for He made male and female and no one yet has found a better pattern for marriage than this. I know that I willingly yield myself when I feel fully loved by my husband.

The Christian life is, as I have said, not static, but a dynamic on-going experience under the sovereignty of God. If we truly do our best to walk in His paths we shall have many exciting revelations on the way. So it was after I was baptised in the Holy Spirit that God helped in an area of my life with which I was having particular difficulty. This was the fact that I had never accepted myself as myself and was always wishing I was someone else. At one period in my depression, I positively disliked myself! I was always wishing I could be like one woman who could play the piano so beautifully, or like another who could sing, or another who could speak or pray so effectively. I wished I had the self-confidence of so many others. 'I have so few natural gifts,' I thought, when I looked at the lives of others!

Then our parish had a week-end away at Fellowship house (now the Lamb of God Community) near Brentwood. The speaker was the Rev. Harold Parkes. It was during one of his sessions of teaching about the sovereignty of God in our creation (Eph. 1) that I was able, for the first time in my life, to say 'Thank you Lord, for making *me*!' What a relief! I saw myself in a new, wonderful way and was truly able to love myself. This in turn released me more fully to love others, for as Jesus had said I could 'love my neighbour *as* I love myself' with a depth before unknown to me.

My faith had not always been positive but I found it to be much more so after I was baptised in the Holy Spirit. The Palmers, Shilcocks and Porters had been given me by God to look after my growing Christian life, but these dear people had, in the main, negative attitudes towards life in this world and passed their views on to me. I was told that the local street-fair in Stamford was today's 'Vanity Fair' and I grew up as a Christian with negative views about such things as dancing, make-up, an occasional drink of alcohol and so on—the whole puritanical list.

I have since learned that just as I can have a positive attitude towards myself, I can have a good outlook on my life in the world and be held secure by Him within it. I love life—every bit of it! I enjoy every day. I don't any longer live by a list of 'thou shalt nots' because I am under grace not legalism. I love God and obey the prompting of His Spirit. We live in a world of God's creating and there is so much good in it. My life now is lived in the spirit of Paul's words: 'Whatsoever things are true, whatsoever things are honest, whatsoever things are just, whatsoever things are pure, whatsoever things are lovely, whatsoever things are of good report. . . think on these things' (Phil. 4:8). It's so good to live in God's world under His sovereignty.

My personal devotions are likewise in no way legalistic. I realise that others may function differently, for instance in having their 'Quiet Times', and they must follow the way God has led them. My times of devotion, however, are in no way fixed. Rarely do I spend long periods of time in prayer like Trevor does. However, I come aside whenever I feel so moved, to talk to Him, read his word and listen to Him. I often sing hymns and spiritual songs whilst walking to town, or in the countryside, as well as when washing-up or cleaning the house. Trevor and I pray together and sometimes read the Bible together, but these are not at fixed times, but are usually spontaneous, over coffee at mid-morning, or before sleeping, or at any other time, especially in a crisis or with an urgent prayer request. It's lovely to be so free in one's relationship with one's Heavenly Father!

My sense of God's sovereignty has helped through what could have been pitfalls in my life in the Charismatic movement. This has been especially so in my experience of the gifts of the Spirit (1 Cor. 12). I saw from the beginning that the Scriptures taught that God would distribute gifts according to *his* will. So, whilst I was always available to be used by God, I did not get concerned when I didn't speak in tongues until several years after I received the laying-on-of-hands for the baptism in the Holy Spirit. I just waited for God's time. Eventually, I found myself praying in tongues for a sick person when I just didn't know what English words to use! Previously, I had been willing at Trevor's request to step forward to minister to the sick, believing it was God's moment and His call upon my life. It has been the same with all the other gifts I have used. I surrender to His will.

I stress even more the 'fruit of the Spirit' (Gal. 5:22) these days, for I am sure that He wants us to exhibit more and more of the character of Jesus in love, peace, patience, kindness, goodness, meekness, and humility, even more than He wants to use us in his gifts. Here too, as we realise that the calling is so high, we can be sure of his sovereign work in us—that He will present us whole in body, soul and spirit before the Father's throne. Faithful is He who has called us, who also will do it (1 Thess. 5).

15: Called to be a Wife

In June 1982 Trevor and I celebrated our Silver Wedding Anniversary with services of thanksgiving and parties both in America and Britain. At our request, Father Richard O'Driscoll, Trevor's assistant at St. Luke's, took us through a re-affirmation of our marriage vows. In America we shared our celebrations with Terry and Janet Biggart—Terry was the Churchwarden who initiated our going to America. In England we ministered at a Power, Praise and Healing Service in the Barn Hill Methodist Church, ministering to the sick on the very spot where twenty-five years earlier we had been joined together as man and wife.

It seems that mid-life is as good a place as any to pause for reflection, especially about what God has taught me about being called to be a wife. Look back with me beyond the day of my marriage to ponder the privilege of being born into this world as a woman.

I often say to Trevor, 'God made no mistake when He created me a woman. With all due respect, I just wouldn't ever have wanted to be a man!' Shouldn't we women always praise God for our femininity! It is only then that we shall be able properly to relate to men and truly enjoy their company, especially Christian men of our own age. We should thank God for our female bodies; for the joy of being able to give birth to children; for being able to think, feel and behave naturally as women. There is no need to regard ourselves as in competition with men or, for that matter, even to begin to identify with the extremes of feminism and the strident elements of the 'women's lib' movements of the present day.

What is more, the converse will also be true, and men will more easily be able to relate to us and treat us as women, because their own manhood is not being threatened. We will, as the Bible says (1 Pet. 3:7), always be treated for what we are physically, the 'weaker vessels'. We will be able in our femininity to 'flow' naturally with men in social life, in Christian fellowship and, when so called of God, be able to relate to our husbands beautifully together as one in Christian ministry. Trevor has often told me that, like many men, he can't cope with women who 'come on strong', especially in Christian ministry, and that he wants to 'run a mile' from them because they seem to want to act the part of a man, rather than exhibiting the true, gentle grace of womanhood. Nevertheless, although women may be physically weaker than men, I am sure that we are frequently *emotionally* the stronger. Hence our ability to support our husbands in times of illness or worry and hence,also, those rewarding words our seemingly grown-up children often surprise us with, when they say, 'Mum, I couldn't manage without you.'

Another important aspect of femininity is that we women should pay proper attention to our appearance, for in this way we can complement the Gospel of our Lord Jesus Christ. Women, my husband tells me, were made to adorn the earth and, like flowers, make it ever more beautiful. As long as I can remember I have paid a lot of attention to my appearance, even in days when we were very short of money. It doesn't mean going to a lot of expense to make oneself as lovely to look at as possible and so adorn the Faith. We must keep our bodies in the best possible shape, and this means paying attention to diet, and it often involves discipline with food especially in middle life.

Although I had always tried to dress smartly, it took the American ladies to teach me about the correct colours for different skin textures. The 'Colour Me Beautiful' (Carole Jackson) phenomenon swept through St. Luke's while I was there and the colour revolution I went through, I am told, brought my features to life in a remarkable way. Of course, as the Scriptures teach us (1 Peter 3) we must not go to extremes in 'outward adornments' and I certainly don't like to see women over-made-up or dressed for show. However, that doesn't mean that Christian women should look dour or dull. It doesn't cost any more money to use the right cosmetics and dress in the right colours than to use the wrong ones. I am so glad, that after I have been sitting for long periods on platforms at meetings with Trevor, women as well as men have complimented me on the fact that I have looked elegant and by my appearance preached a Gospel of peace and joy.

Although I am by profession a nurse, I have not actually nursed anyone other than Trevor for many years. I would need a refresher course before I could ever start again. However, I have no intention of doing this as I am so involved in our joint renewal ministry. So I have found myself describing my occupation on legal documents as 'a housewife' or, as Americans would say, 'a homemaker'. It took the Lord a long time to get through to me that this is the highest calling to which any woman can respond this side of eternity. Since I came to see this I have recalled that the Bible states that Eve was created for this very purpose. The Book of Proverbs paints a picture of the ideal woman as a highly efficient housewife. We must remember, however, that such a calling very much includes being a 'help-meet' to our husbands. Of course, modern domestic appliances have made it possible for the housework to be done far more speedily and efficiently than ever before and many women, therefore, do have another occupation. I am certainly grateful for my share in the evangelistic missions in which I find such fulfilment.

However, it is my opinion, from my own experience, that a woman should put her home and family *first* in her occupations, especially while her children still need her to be at home when they are not at school, or when they come home from work. Her husband, too, although these days so often a partner in doing household chores, should be ministered to by his wife and come first on her list of priorities. One of the main reasons for domestic strife and neglected children is that so many women are failing to see that being a housewife is our highest calling from God. Of course, some women, the minority, are called to remain unmarried, or do so by accident, and these wonderful people can serve the Lord more freely in other ways. Single people *can* find *complete* fulfilment, for instance as pastoral assistants in the Church, or as social workers, in child care, as old people's wardens, as well as in many other 'secular' occupations, often in positions of much responsibility.

Trevor and I have had the privilege of staying in many homes where all I have conceived about a woman's calling has been evident. These have, in the vast majority of cases, been happy homes. Sadly we have also known cases where the woman of the house has clearly rejected or been resentful of her call to be a housewife, regarding it as a chore rather than a high calling. Perhaps some of these women have lacked caring and grateful husbands. Certainly they need to be affirmed by their spouses and Churches in their high calling as the family's homemaker.

I have always felt that a woman's home, like her outward appearance, should reflect the glory of the Gospel of Jesus. We should, therefore give a great deal of time and thought to the interior decoration of our homes. I have found this to be possible even though we have moved house so frequently, I have managed to do it without a great deal of expense. I have been thrilled when visitors have complimented me about my taste in house-furnishings and the sense of peace which has pervaded the house, just through the way in which it has been furnished and decorated. Surely, even if we cannot afford a lot in the way of antiques or brand new furniture, we Christian women should always make sure that our homes are clean, as befits saints! Of course, one must avoid such obsessions with tidiness that makes the family uneasy or nervous about playing, entertaining or even being in their home. Nevertheless, surely 'cleanliness is next to godliness' not only in personal hygiene but in the state of a Christian's home. Let us glorify God in our hearts, in our appearance and in our homes. As John Keble so rightly said:

If on our daily course our mind
Be set to hallow all we find,
New treasures still, of countless price,
God will provide for sacrifice.

The trivial round, the common task,
Will furnish all we ought to ask—
Room to deny ourselves, a road
To bring us daily nearer God.

For myself, as for most Christian women, being a housewife has meant, with my husband, seeking to bring up our children in the 'nuture and admonition of the Lord'. As Methodists and then Anglicans, we took our four children for baptism very soon after they were born. I do not think that their eternal destiny was in any way affected by that act done for them by Christian parents and godparents. I do believe, however, that in the deepest way we were giving our children back to God for His providential care and keeping. I believe that, on account of our faith as parents, they were covered from that time by the Sacrificial blood of Jesus. As an evangelical Christian, however, I know that this act was a sort of holding operation, awaiting the day of their own personal decision to commit themselves to Christ. I am grateful to God that they have all done this.

I am indeed grateful because I think life for the children of Christian ministers can be very difficult. They can have so much 'religion' thrust upon them, and so much expected of them by parents and parishioners, that they can be put off Christianity for life. In fact, our own children were never forced to go to Church after they had reached the age of about seven. They were of course *encouraged* to attend Church because, as we explained, it was the most important event that we ever did as a family together. However, we always made the week-end a 'fun' time and Sunday, as far as

Trevor's duties allowed, a 'fun' day. So we would spend time between services at the local park for a family time together. I have become of the opinion that Christian families should only attend one service on a Sunday, after the American pattern, and then have the rest of the day as a family day.

So our children felt part of the Church from their earliest days and even sometimes attended Power, Praise and Healing Services at St. Paul's, Hainault, on Tuesday evenings. We never pressed them about making a Christian commitment because we realised that true conversion could never be the result of parental pressure, only a work of the Holy Spirit in His own time and way. Rebecca gave her heart to the Lord at a youth Pathfinder gathering, Ruth at a Billy Graham Rally, Rachael at a mission to children in a neighbouring Church, and Philip spoke in other tongues when he was seven years of age!

During adolescence we never placed rigid restrictions on the life of any of our children. They all grew up as Christians within the world and were not over-protected or cushioned from it. They enjoyed all the pleasures of growing up with a positive attitude to life and we left them to experience the 'world', being ever ready with advice, and even help when they experienced its hardships and let-downs. They found their own way to Jesus, like we did, through their own experience of life, and their Christian upbringing never deserted or failed them. At times, of course, we had to 'hang on with spiritually bated breath' at some of the things they got up to. Nevertheless none of them has ever been in moral or legal trouble. They behaved themselves freely, happily, but well. They did not go on drugs or into any of the devil's traps. We thank God for the beautiful, open relationship we have always enjoyed with them, for the love they have said they have always felt to be abounding for them and for our Christian arms ever ready to receive them. We are proud of them and frequently during every year, now they are fully grown, they say they thank God for their parents; as Rachael wrote to me one day, 'Thank you, Mum, for bringing me into the world, and above all thank you for bringing me up a Christian.'

Such words are a delight, together with the way Trevor so frequently takes me into his arms, looks into my eyes, and from the depth of his heart says, 'Thank you, darling, I love you, you are the best wife a man ever could have. I love you and I am grateful, and daily thank God for you.' So I am fulfilled and thankful myself that God called me to be a wife.